Fat Chance—
The Chemistry of Lipids

Developed in collaboration with

Henkel Corporation, Emery Group

Series Editor
Mickey Sarquis, Director
Center for Chemical Education

This project was supported, in part, by the National Science Foundation. Any opinions, findings, and conclusions or recommendations expressed in this material are those of the authors and do not necessarily reflect the views of the National Science Foundation. The Government has certain rights to this material. This material is based upon work supported by the National Science Foundation under Grant No. TPE-9153930.

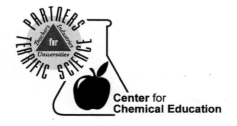

**Center for
Chemical Education**

This monograph is intended for use by teachers, chemists, and properly supervised students. Teachers and other users must develop and follow procedures for the safe handling, use, and disposal of chemicals in accordance with local and state regulations and requirements. The cautions, warnings, and safety reminders associated with the doing of experiments and activities involving the use of chemicals and equipment contained in this publication have been compiled from sources believed to be reliable and to represent the best opinion on the subject as of 1995. However, no warranty, guarantee, or representation is made by the editor, contributors, Henkel Corporation, or the Terrific Science Press as to the correctness or sufficiency of any information herein. Neither the editor, contributors, Henkel Corporation, nor the Terrific Science Press assumes any responsibility or liability for the use of the information herein, nor can it be assumed that all necessary warnings and precautionary measures are contained in this publication. Other or additional information or measures may be required or desirable because of particular or exceptional conditions or circumstances, or because of new or changed legislation.

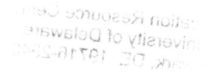

Contributors

Industrial Mentor

Tim Cassady
Research Organic Chemist, Henkel Corporation, Emery Group
Cincinnati, Ohio

Academic Mentor

John Alexander
Chemistry Department, University of Cincinnati
Cincinnati, Ohio

Peer Mentors

Rebecca Stricklin
Chemistry Teacher, Oak Hills High School
Cincinnati, Ohio

Marian Moeckel
Teacher, Edgewood High School
Trenton, Ohio

Principal Investigators

Mickey Sarquis	Miami University, Middletown, Ohio
Jim Coats	Dow Chemical USA (retired), Findlay, Ohio
Dan McLoughlin	Xavier University, Cincinnati, Ohio
Rex Bucheit	Fillmore Elementary School, Hamilton, Ohio

Partners for Terrific Science Advisory Board

Ruby L. Bryant	Colonel White High School, Dayton, Ohio
Rex Bucheit	Fillmore Elementary School (ex-officio), Hamilton, Ohio
Jim Coats	Dow Chemical USA (retired, ex-officio), Findlay, Ohio
Dick French	Quantum Chemical Corporation (retired, ex-officio), Cincinnati, Ohio
Judy Gilbert	BP America/Ohio Chemical Council, Lima, Ohio
Linda Jester	John XXIII Elementary School, Middletown, Ohio
James C. Letton	Procter & Gamble, Cincinnati, Ohio
Ted J. Logan	Procter & Gamble, Ross, Ohio
Ken Lohr	Hoechst Marion Roussel, Inc. (retired), Cincinnati, Ohio
Alan McClelland	Delaware Science Alliance (DuPont, retired), Rockland, Delaware (deceased)
Dan McLoughlin	Xavier University (ex-officio), Cincinnati, Ohio
Raymond C. Odioso	R.C. Odioso Consultants, Inc. (Drackett, retired), Cincinnati, Ohio, St. Petersburg Beach, Florida
Tom Runyan	Garfield Alternative School, Middletown, Ohio
Ken Wilkinson	Hilton Davis Company (retired), Cincinnati, Ohio
John P. Williams	Miami University Hamilton, Hamilton, Ohio
Regina Wolterman	Our Lady of Lourdes Elementary School, Cincinnati, Ohio

Table of Contents

Contributors .... *iii*

Principal Investigators .... *iv*

Partners for Terrific Science Advisory Board .... *iv*

Acknowledgments .... *vi*

Foreword .... *vii*

The Center for Chemical Education .... *viii*

Partnership Network .... *xii*

An Invitation to Industrial Chemists .... *xiii*

How to Use This Teacher Resource Module *1*

Employing Appropriate Safety Procedures *3*

Background for Teachers *6*
    Overview of the Oleochemical Industry 6
    The Emery Group of Henkel Corporation 6
    Content Review 7

Using the Activities in the Classroom *15*
    Pedagogical Strategies 15
    Annotated List of Activities and Demonstrations 16
    Curriculum Placement Guide 17

Activities and Demonstrations *19*
    1. Esters 21
    2. Making Candles 27
    3. Candle Investigations 33
    4. Making Cleansing Cream 41
    5. Preparation and Comparison of Four Soaps 47
    6. Surface Tension 57
    7. Blowing Bubbles 65
    8. Food Colors in Milk 71
    9. Emulsifying Peanut or Vegetable Oil 77
    10. Properties of Lubricants 83
    11. Make-It-Yourself Slime 91

Acknowledgments

The authors and editor wish to thank the following individuals who have contributed to the development of the *Science in Our World* series of Teacher Resource Modules.

Terrific Science Press Design and Production Team
Susan Gertz, Amy Stander, Lisa Taylor, Thomas Nackid, Stephen Gentle, Vickie Fultz, Anne Munson, Amy Hudepohl, Andrea Nolan, Pamela Mason

Reviewers
Frank Cardulla	Niles North High School, Skokie, Illinois
Susan Hershberger	Miami University, Oxford, Ohio
Naomi Horchak-Morris	Indian Hill High School, Cincinnati, Ohio
Baird Lloyd	Miami University, Middletown, Ohio
Mark Sabo	Miami University, Middletown, Ohio
Dave Tomlin	Wright Patterson Air Force Base, Dayton, Ohio
Linda Woodward	University of Southwestern Louisiana, Lafayette, Louisiana

Center for Chemical Education Staff

Mickey Sarquis, Director
Bruce L. Peters, Jr., Associate Director
Billie Gerzema, Administrative Assistant

Assistants to Director
Susan Gertz	Mark Sabo
Lynn Hogue	Lisa Meeder Turnbull

Project Coordinators and Managers
Richard French	Andrea Nolan
Betty Kibbey	Ginger Smith
Carl Morgan	Amy Stander

Research Associates and Assistants
Kersti Cox	Pamela Mason
Stephen Gentle	Anne Munson
Susan Hershberger	Thomas Nackid
Amy Hudepohl	Michael Parks
Robert Hunter	Lisa Taylor

Program Secretaries
Victoria Burton	Ruth Willis

Graduate Assistants
Michelle Diebolt	Richard Rischling
Nancy Grim	Michella Stultz

Foreword

Fat Chance—The Chemistry of Lipids is one of the *Science in Our World* Teacher Resource Modules. This set is aimed at enabling teachers to introduce their students to the concepts and processes of industrial chemistry and relate these concepts to the consumer products students encounter daily. These hands-on, problem-solving activities help connect science lessons with real life.

Developed as a collaborative effort between industrial, academic, and teacher peer mentors in the *Partners for Terrific Science* program, this module provides background information on the oleochemical industry and Henkel Corporation, Emery Group's role in this industry, as well as a content review of oleochemistry and pedagogical strategies. The activities in this module have been tested by participants in *Partners* programs and by *Partners* teachers in their classrooms, and reviewed by experts in the field to help ensure accuracy, safety, and pedagogical effectiveness.

Partners for Terrific Science, established in 1986, is an industrial/academic partnership that facilitates interaction among classroom teachers, industrial scientists and engineers, and university chemistry faculty to make science education more interesting, relevant, and understandable for all students. The partnership is supported by the Ohio Chemical Council and its more than 100 members, the National Science Foundation, the U.S. Department of Education, the Ohio Board of Regents, the American Chemical Society—Cincinnati Section, Miami University, and over 50 private-sector partners. Henkel Corporation, Emery Group has generously contributed to the production of this module.

The Teacher Resource Modules have been developed especially for teachers who want to use industry-based physical science activities in the classroom, but who may not have been able to attend a *Partners* workshop at the Miami site or one of the Affiliate sites nationwide. We want to thank all the contributors, participants, and mentors who made this publication possible.

We hope you will find that these Teacher Resource Modules provide you with a useful and exciting way to involve your students in doing chemistry through integrated real-world themes. We welcome your comments at any time and are interested in learning about especially successful uses of these materials.

Mickey Sarquis, Director
Center for Chemical Education
July 1995

The Center for Chemical Education

Built on a tradition of quality programming, materials development, and networking between academia and industry, Miami University's Center for Chemical Education (CCE) encompasses a multifaceted collaboration of cross-grade-level and interdisciplinary initiatives begun in the mid-1980s as Terrific Science Programs. These initiatives are linked through the centrality of chemistry to the goal of fostering quality hands-on, minds-on science education for all students. CCE activities include credit coursework and other opportunities for educators at all levels; K–12 student programs; undergraduate, graduate, and postgraduate programs in chemical education; materials development, including teacher resource materials, program handbooks, and videos; public outreach efforts and networking to foster new and existing partnerships among classroom teachers, university-based science educators, industrial scientists, and professional societies.

Professional Development for Educators

Credit Courses
: The Center for Chemical Education offers a variety of summer and academic-year workshop-style courses for K–12 and college teachers. While each workshop has a unique focus, all reflect current pedagogical approaches in science education, cutting-edge academic and industrial research topics, and classroom applications for teachers and students. Short courses provide opportunities for educators to enrich their science teaching in a limited amount of time. All courses offer graduate credit.

Non-Credit Courses
: Academies allow CCE graduates and other teachers to attend special one-day sessions presented by leading science educators from around the United States. Offerings include seminars, mini-workshops, and share-and-swap sessions.

Internships
: Through 8- to 10-week summer internships, program graduates work as members of industrial teams to gain insight into the day-to-day workings of industrial laboratories, enabling them to bring real-world perspectives into the classroom.

Fellowships
: Master teachers at primary, secondary, and college levels do research in chemical education and undertake curriculum and materials development as Teacher Fellows with the Center for Chemical Education. Fellowships are available for the summer and the academic year.

K–12 Student Programming

Summer Camps
: A variety of summer camps are available to area elementary, middle, and high school students. These camps not only provide laboratory-based enrichment for students, but also enable educators in summer courses to apply their knowledge of hands-on exploration and leadership skills. Satellite camps are offered at affiliated sites throughout the country.

Science Carnivals
: Carnivals challenge elementary school students with hands-on science in a non-traditional atmosphere, encouraging them to apply the scientific method to activities that demonstrate scientific principles. Sponsoring teachers and their students host these carnivals for other students in their districts.

Super Saturday Science Sessions	High school students are introduced to industrial and research applications of science and technology through special Saturday sessions that involve the students in experiment-based problem-solving. Topics have included waste management, environmental sampling, engineering technology, paper science, chemical analysis, microbiology, and many others.
Ambassador Program	Professional chemists, technicians, and engineers, practicing and recently retired, play important roles as classroom ambassadors for high school and two-year college students. Ambassadors not only serve as classroom resources, but they are also available as consultants when a laboratory scenario calls for outside expertise; they mentor special projects both in and out of the classroom; and they are available for career counseling and professional advice.

Undergraduate and Graduate Student Programming

Teaching Science with TOYS Undergraduate Course	This undergraduate course replicates the Teaching Science with TOYS teacher inservice program for the preservice audience. Students participate in hands-on physics and chemistry sessions.
General Chemistry Initiative	This effort is aimed at more effectively including chemical analysis and problem solving in the two-year college curriculum. To accomplish this goal, we are developing and testing discovery-based laboratory scenarios and take-home lecture supplements that illustrate topics in chemistry through activities beyond the classroom. In addition to demonstrating general chemistry concepts, these activities also involve students in critical-thinking and group problem-solving skills used by professional chemists in industry and academia.
Chemical Technology Curriculum Development	Curriculum and materials development efforts highlight the collaboration between college and high school faculty and industrial partners. These efforts will lead to the dissemination of a series of activity-based monographs, including detailed instructions for discovery-based investigations that challenge students to apply principles of chemical technology, chemical analysis, and Good Laboratory Practices in solving problems that confront practicing chemical technicians in the workplace.
Other Undergraduate Activities	The CCE has offered short courses/seminars for undergraduates that are similar in focus and pedagogy to CCE teacher/faculty enhancement programming. In addition, CCE staff members provide Miami University students with opportunities to interact in area schools through public outreach efforts and to undertake independent study projects in chemical education.
Degree Program	Miami's Department of Chemistry offers both a Ph.D. and M.S. in Chemical Education for graduate students who are interested in becoming teachers of chemistry in situations where a comprehensive knowledge of advanced chemical concepts is required and where acceptable scholarly activity can include the pursuit of chemical education research.

Educational Materials

The Terrific Science Press publications have emerged from CCE's work with classroom teachers of grades K–12 and college in graduate-credit, workshop-style inservice courses. Before being released, our materials undergo extensive classroom testing by teachers working with students at the targeted grade level, peer review by experts in the field for accuracy and safety, and editing by a staff of technical writers for clear, accurate, and consistent materials lists and procedures. The following is a list of Terrific Science Press publications to date.

Science Activities
for Elementary Classrooms
(1986)

Science SHARE is a resource for busy K–6 teachers to enable them to use hands-on science activities in their classrooms. The activities included use common, everyday materials and complement or supplement any existing science curriculum. This book was published in collaboration with Flinn Scientific, Inc.

Polymers All Around You!
(1992)

This monograph focuses on the uses of polymer chemistry in the classroom. It includes several multi-part activities dealing with topics such as polymer recycling and polymers and polarized light. This monograph was published in collaboration with POLYED, a joint education committee of two divisions of the American Chemical Society: the Division of Polymer Chemistry and the Division of the Polymeric Materials: Science and Engineering.

Fun with Chemistry
Volume 2
(1993)

The second volume of a set of two hands-on activity collections, this book contains classroom-tested science activities that enhance teaching, are fun to do, and help make science relevant to young students. This book was published in collaboration with the Institute for Chemical Education (ICE), University of Wisconsin-Madison.

Santa's Scientific Christmas
(1993)

In this school play for elementary students, Santa's elves teach him the science behind his toys. The book and accompanying video provide step-by-step instructions for presenting the play. The book also contains eight fun, hands-on science activities to do in the classroom.

Teaching Chemistry with TOYS
Teaching Physics with TOYS
(1995)

Each volume contains more than 40 activities for grades K–9. Both were developed in collaboration with and tested by classroom teachers from around the country. These volumes were published in collaboration with McGraw-Hill, Inc.

Palette of Color
Monograph Series
(1995)

The three monographs in this series present the chemistry behind dye colors and show how this chemistry is applied in "real-world" settings:
- The Chemistry of Vat Dyes
- The Chemistry of Natural Dyes
- The Chemistry of Food Dyes

Science in Our World
Teacher Resource Modules
(1995)

Each volume of this five-volume set presents chemistry activities based on a specific industry—everything from pharmaceuticals to polymers. Developed as a result of the *Partners for Terrific Science* program, this set explores the following topics and industries:
- Science Fare—Chemistry at the Table (Procter & Gamble)
- Strong Medicine—Chemistry at the Pharmacy (Hoechst Marion Roussel, Inc.)
- Dirt Alert—The Chemistry of Cleaning (Diversey Corporation)
- Fat Chance—The Chemistry of Lipids (Henkel Corporation, Emery Group)
- Chain Gang—The Chemistry of Polymers (Quantum Chemical Corporation)

Teaching Physical Science through Children's Literature (1996)	This book offers 20 complete lessons for teaching hands-on, discovery-oriented physical science in the elementary classroom using children's fiction and nonfiction books as an integral part of that instruction. Each lesson in this book is a tightly integrated learning episode with a clearly defined science content objective supported and enriched by all facets of the lesson, including reading of both fiction and nonfiction, writing, and, where appropriate, mathematics. Along with the science content objectives, many process objectives are woven into every lesson.
Teaching Science with TOYS Teacher Resource Modules (1996, 1997)	The modules in this series are designed as instructional units focusing on a given theme or content area in chemistry or physics. Built around a collection of grade-level-appropriate TOYS activities, each Teacher Resource Module also includes a content review and pedagogical strategies section. Volumes listed below were published or are forthcoming in collaboration with McGraw-Hill, Inc. • Exploring Matter with TOYS: Using and Understanding the Senses • Investigating Solids, Liquids, and Gases with TOYS: States of Matter and Changes of State • Transforming Energy with TOYS: Mechanical Energy and Energy Conversions

Terrific Science Network

Affiliates	College and district affiliates to CCE programs disseminate ideas and programming throughout the United States. Program affiliates offer support for local teachers, including workshops, resource/symposium sessions, and inservices; science camps; and college courses.
Industrial Partners	We collaborate directly with over 40 industrial partners, all of whom are fully dedicated to enhancing the quality of science education for teachers and students in their communities and beyond. A list of corporations and organizations that support *Partners for Terrific Science* is included on the following page.
Outreach	On the average, graduates of CCE professional development programs report reaching about 40 other teachers through district inservices and other outreach efforts they undertake. Additionally, graduates, especially those in facilitator programs, institute their own local student programs. CCE staff also undertake significant outreach through collaboration with local schools, service organizations, professional societies, and museums.
Newsletters	CCE newsletters provide a vehicle for network communication between program graduates, members of industry, and other individuals active in chemical and science education. Newsletters contain program information, hands-on science activities, teacher resources, and ideas on how to integrate hands-on science into the curriculum.

For more information about any of the CCE initiatives, contact us at

Center for Chemical Education
4200 East University Blvd.
Middletown, OH 45042
513/727-3318
FAX: 513/727-3223
e-mail: *CCE@muohio.edu*
http://www.muohio.edu/~ccecwis/

Partnership Network

We appreciate the dedication and contributions of the following corporations and organizations, who together make *Partners for Terrific Science* a true partnership for the betterment of chemical education for all teachers and students.

Partners in the Private Sector

A & B Foundry, Inc.
Aeronca, Inc.
Ag Renu
Air Products and Chemicals, Inc.
Armco, Inc.
Armco Research and Technology
ARW Polywood
Ashland Chemical Company
Bank One
BASF
Bay West Paper Corporation
Black Clawson Company
BP America: BP Oil, BP Chemicals
Coats & Clark
Crystal Tissue Company
DataChem Laboratories, Inc.
Diversey Corporation
Ronald T. Dodge Company
Dover Chemical Corporation
Dow Chemical USA
Fluor Daniel Fernald, Inc.
Formica
Henkel Corporation, Emery Group

Hewlett-Packard Company
Hilton Davis Company
Hoechst Marion Roussel, Inc.
Inland Container Corporation
Jefferson Smurfit Corporation
JLJ, Inc.
Magnode Corporation
Middletown Paperboard Corporation
Middletown Regional Hospital
Middletown Wastewater Treatment Plant
Middletown Water Treatment Plant
Miller Brewing Company
The Monsanto Fund
Owens Corning Science & Technology Laboratories
The Procter & Gamble Company
Quality Chemicals
Quantum Chemical Corporation
Rumpke Waste Removal/Recycling
Shepherd Chemical Company
Shepherd Color Company
Sorg Paper Company
Square D Company
Sun Chemical Corporation

Partners in the Public Sector

Hamilton County Board of Education
Indiana Tech-Prep
Miami University
Middletown Clean Community
National Institute of Environmental Health Sciences
National Science Foundation
Ohio Board of Regents, Columbus, OH

Ohio Department of Education
Ohio Environmental Protection Agency
Ohio Tech-Prep
State Board for Technical and Comprehensive Education, Columbia, SC
US Department of Education
US Department of Energy, Cincinnati, OH

Professional Societies

American Association of Physics Teachers
African American Math-Science Coalition
American Chemical Society— Central Regional Council
American Chemical Society— Cincinnati Section
American Chemical Society— Dayton Section
American Chemical Society—POLYED
American Chemical Society— Technician Division
American Chemical Society, Washington, DC

American Institute of Chemical Engineers
Chemical Manufacturers Association
Chemistry Teachers Club of New York
Intersocietal Polymer and Plastics Education Initiative
Minorities in Mathematics, Science and Engineering
National Organization of Black Chemists and Chemical Engineers—Cincinnati Section
National Science Teachers Association
Ohio Chemical Council
Science Education Council of Ohio
Society of Plastics Engineers

More than 3,000 teachers are involved in and actively benefiting from this Network.

An Invitation to Industrial Chemists

It is not unusual to hear children say they want to be doctors, astronauts, or teachers when they grow up. It is easy for children to see adults they admire doing these jobs in books, on television, and in real life. But where are our aspiring chemists? The chemist portrayed on television often bears close resemblance to Mr. Hyde: an unrealistic and unfortunate role model.

Children delight in learning and enjoy using words like "stegosaurus" and "pterodactyl." Wouldn't it be wonderful to hear words like "chromatography" and "density" used with the same excitement? You could be introducing elementary school students to these words for the first time. And imagine a 10-year-old child coming home from school and announcing, "When I grow up, I want to be a chemist!" You can be the one responsible for such enthusiasm. By taking the time to visit and interact with an elementary or middle school classroom as a guest scientist, you can become the chemist who makes the difference.

You are probably aware that many non-chemists, including many prehigh school teachers, find science in general (and chemistry in particular) mysterious and threatening. When given a chance, both teachers and students can enjoy transforming the classroom into a laboratory and exploring like real scientists. Consider being the catalyst for this transformation.

Unlike magicians, scientists attempt to find explanations for why and how things happen. Challenge students to join in on the fun of searching for explanations. At the introductory level, it is far more important to provide non-threatening opportunities for the students to postulate "why?" than it is for their responses to be absolutely complete. If the accepted explanation is too complex to discuss, maybe the emphasis of the presentation is wrong. For example, discussions focusing on the fact that a color change can be an indication of a chemical reaction may be more useful than a detailed explanation of the reaction mechanisms involved.

Because science involves the process of discovery, it is equally important to let the students know that not all the answers are known and that they too can make a difference. Teachers should be made to feel that responses like "I don't know. What do you think?" or "Let's find out together," are acceptable. It is also important to point out that not everyone's results will be the same. Reinforce the idea that a student's results are not wrong just because they are different from a classmate's results.

While using the term "chemistry," try relating the topics to real-life experiences and integrating topics into non-science areas. After all, chemistry is all around us, not just in the chemistry lab.

When interacting with students, take care to involve all of them. It is very worthwhile to spend time talking informally with small groups or individual students before, during, or after your presentation. It is important to convey the message that chemistry is for all who are willing to apply themselves to the questions before them. Chemistry is neither sexist, racist, nor frightening.

For more information on becoming involved in the classroom and a practical and valuable discussion of some do's and don'ts, a resource is available. The American Chemical Society Education Division has an informative booklet and video called *Chemists in the Classroom*. You may request this package for $20.00 from: ACS Education Division, American Chemical Society, 1155 Sixteenth Street NW, Washington, DC 20036, 800/227-5558.

How to Use This Teacher Resource Module

This section is an introduction to the Teacher Resource Module and its organization. The industry featured in this module is the oleochemical industry.

How Is This Resource Module Organized?

The Teacher Resource Module is organized into the following main sections: How to Use This Teacher Resource Module (this section), Background for Teachers, Using the Activities in the Classroom, and Activities and Demonstrations. Background for Teachers includes Overview of the Oleochemical Industry, The Emery Group of Henkel Corporation, and Content Review. Using the Activities in the Classroom includes Pedagogical Strategies, an Annotated List of Activities and Demonstrations, and a Curriculum Placement Guide. The following paragraphs provide a brief overview of the *Fat Chance—The Chemistry of Lipids* module.

Background for Teachers

Overviews of the oleochemical industry and Henkel Corporation, Emery Group's role in the industry provide information to help you feature the industrial focus of these activities in the classroom. The Content Review section is intended to provide you, the teacher, with an introduction to (or a review of) the concepts covered in the module. The material in this section (and in the individual activity explanations) intentionally gives you information at a level beyond what you will present to your students. You can then evaluate how to adjust the content presentation for your own students.

The Content Review section in this module covers the following topics:
- Fats and Oils: An Introduction
- Fats and Oils as Raw Materials
- Soap-Making
- Lubricants

Using the Activities in the Classroom

The Pedagogical Strategies section provides ideas for effectively teaching a unit on the oleochemical industry. It suggests a variety of ways to incorporate the industry-based activities presented in the module into your curriculum. The Annotated List of Activities and Demonstrations and the Curriculum Placement Guide provide recommended grade levels, descriptions of the activities, and recommended placement of the activities within a typical curriculum.

Module Activities

Each module activity includes complete instructions for conducting the activity in your classroom. These activities have been classroom-tested by teachers like yourself and have been demonstrated to be practical, safe, and effective in the typical classroom. The following information is provided for each activity:

Recommended Grade Level: The grade levels at which the activity will be most effective are listed.

Group Size: The optimal student group size is listed.

Time for Preparation:	This includes time to set up for the activity before beginning with the students.
Time for Procedure:	An estimated time for conducting the activity is listed. This time estimate is based on feedback from classroom testing, but your time may vary depending on your classroom and teaching style.
Materials:	Materials are listed for each part of the activity, divided into amounts per class, per group, and per student.
Resources:	Sources for difficult-to-find materials are listed.
Safety and Disposal:	Special safety and/or disposal procedures are listed if required.
Getting Ready:	Information is provided in Getting Ready when preparation is needed prior to beginning the activity with the students.
Opening Strategy:	A strategy for introducing the topic to be covered and for gaining the students' interest is suggested.
Procedure:	The steps in the Procedure are directed toward you, the teacher, and include cautions and suggestions where appropriate.
Variations and Extensions:	Variations are alternative methods for doing the Procedure. Extensions are methods for furthering student understanding.
Discussion:	Possible questions for students are provided.
Explanation:	The Explanation is written to you, the teacher, and is intended to be modified for students.
Key Science Concepts:	Targeted key science topics are listed.
Cross-Curricular Integration:	Cross-Curricular Integration provides suggestions for integrating the science activity with other areas of the curriculum.
References:	References used to write this activity are listed.

Notes and safety cautions are included in activities as needed and are indicated by the following icons and type style:

Notes are preceded by an arrow.

Cautions are preceded by an exclamation point.

Employing Appropriate Safety Procedures

Experiments, demonstrations, and hands-on activities add relevance, fun, and excitement to science education at any level. However, even the simplest activity can become dangerous when the proper safety precautions are ignored or when the activity is done incorrectly or performed by students without proper supervision. While the activities in this book include cautions, warnings, and safety reminders from sources believed to be reliable, and while the text has been extensively reviewed, it is your responsibility to develop and follow procedures for the safe execution of any activity you choose to do and for the safe handling, use, and disposal of chemicals in accordance with local and state regulations and requirements.

Safety First

- Collect and read the Materials Safety Data Sheets (MSDS) for all of the chemicals used in your experiments. MSDS's provide physical property data, toxicity information, and handling and disposal specifications for chemicals. They can be obtained upon request from manufacturers and distributors of these chemicals. In fact, MSDS's are often shipped with chemicals when they are ordered. These should be collected and made available to students, faculty, or parents for information about specific chemicals in these activities.

- Read and follow the American Chemical Society Minimum Safety Guidelines for Chemical Demonstrations on the next page. Remember that you are a role model for your students—your attention to safety will help them develop good safety habits while assuring that everyone has fun with these activities.

- Read each activity carefully and observe all safety precautions and disposal procedures. Determine and follow all local and state regulations and requirements.

- Never attempt an activity if you are unfamiliar or uncomfortable with the procedures or materials involved. Consult a high school or college chemistry teacher or an industrial chemist for advice or ask him or her to perform the activity for your class. These people are often delighted to help.

- Always practice activities yourself before using them with your class. This is the only way to become thoroughly familiar with an activity, and familiarity will help prevent potentially hazardous (or merely embarrassing) mishaps. In addition, you may find variations that will make the activity more meaningful to your students.

- Undertake activities only at the recommended grade levels and only with adult supervision.

- You, your assistants, and any students participating in the preparation for or doing of the activity must wear safety goggles if indicated in the activity and at any other time you deem necessary.

- Special safety instructions are not given for everyday classroom materials being used in a typical manner. Use common sense when working with hot, sharp, or breakable objects. Keep tables or desks covered to avoid stains. Keep spills cleaned up to avoid falls.

- When an activity requires students to smell a substance, instruct them to smell the substance as follows: hold its container approximately 6 inches from the nose and, using the free hand, gently waft the air above the open container toward the nose. Never smell an unknown substance by placing it directly under the nose. (See figure.)

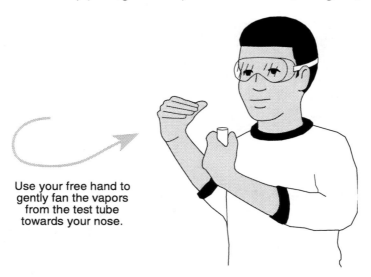

Use your free hand to gently fan the vapors from the test tube towards your nose.

Wafting procedure—Carefully wave the air above the open container towards your nose. Avoid hitting the container in the process.

- Caution students never to taste anything made in the laboratory and not to place their fingers in their mouths after handling laboratory chemicals.

ACS Minimum Safety Guidelines for Chemical Demonstrations

This section outlines safety procedures that Chemical Demonstrators must follow at all times.

1. Know the properties of the chemicals and the chemical reactions involved in all demonstrations presented.

2. Comply with all local rules and regulations.

3. Wear appropriate eye protection for all chemical demonstrations.

4. Warn the members of the audience to cover their ears whenever a loud noise is anticipated.

5. Plan the demonstration so that harmful quantities of noxious gases (e.g., NO_2, SO_2, H_2S) do not enter the local air supply.

6. Provide safety shield protection wherever there is the slightest possibility that a container, its fragments or its contents could be propelled with sufficient force to cause personal injury.

7. Arrange to have a fire extinguisher at hand whenever the slightest possibility for fire exists.

8. Do not taste or encourage spectators to taste any non-food substance.

9. Never use demonstrations in which parts of the human body are placed in danger (such as placing dry ice in the mouth or dipping hands into liquid nitrogen).

10. Do not use "open" containers of volatile, toxic substances (e.g., benzene, CCl_4, CS_2, formaldehyde) without adequate ventilation as provided by fume hoods.

11. Provide written procedure, hazard, and disposal information for each demonstration whenever the audience is encouraged to repeat the demonstration.

12. Arrange for appropriate waste containers for and subsequent disposal of materials harmful to the environment.

Background for Teachers

This Teacher Resource Module, developed as part of the *Partners for Terrific Science* program, provides you, the teacher, with a brief overview of the oleochemical industry, a summary of Henkel Corporation, Emery Group's role in this industry, a Content Review, a Using the Activities in the Classroom section, and a collection of activities and demonstrations.

Overview of the Oleochemical Industry

The oleochemical industry uses both fats and oils as raw materials. The prefix "oleo" signifies oil; the oils discussed in this module are so-called "fixed oils" which are fatty substances from vegetables and animals. These fixed oils contain esters (glycerol triesters) of fatty acids which are liquid at room temperature. Solid or semi-solid esters of fatty acids are referred to as fats, and in the impure form they are called tallow.

Fats and oils are renewable sources—feed stocks that can be replenished by growing more of the plants and animals from which they are extracted. In contrast, resources such as petroleum and coal require oxygen-free (anaerobic) high-temperature and high-pressure conditions for their production. This natural process takes millions of years to occur.

Soap is the most familiar product of the oleochemical industry. However, the properties which make substances good soaps also make them useful for other purposes such as formulating cosmetic and personal care products. Lubricants for automobiles and jet engines, plastics, polymers, candles, waxes, paints, food products, corrosion inhibitors, greases, and detergents also rely on products from the oleochemical industry.

The Emery Group of Henkel Corporation

The Emery Group of Henkel Corporation specializes in oleochemicals. The operations at Emery are designed to extract and purify fatty acids and to modify the structure of these acids or combine them with other substances to produce chemicals for special needs. Glycerol (glycerin) is a valuable by-product of several Henkel processes.

For modifying the structure of some unsaturated fatty acids, the Emery Group produces highly reactive ozone (O_3); worldwide it is the largest producer and user of ozone.

The Emery Group owes its existence to the historic role of Cincinnati as a center for marketing and butchering livestock from the surrounding farming area. Cincinnati's location on the Ohio River allowed both live animals and meat to be shipped conveniently. In 1840, Thomas Emery founded a company which converted meat by-products (which were obtainable at a low cost from local butchering operations) into lard oil for lamps and tallow for candles. (Procter & Gamble also began its Cincinnati operation, in a similar fashion, as a manufacturer of candles.) With the advent of oil drilling and the refining of petroleum which provided kerosene ("coal oil") for burning in lamps, the lard oil business decreased radically in importance. However, Emery still manufactured candles until the 1960s.

Presently Emery provides oleochemicals as raw materials to manufacturers of various kinds of industrial and consumer products. As a result, the Emery name is not seen on labels of consumer products. Table 1 lists some consumer products which are manufactured with Emery oleochemicals.

Product	Emery Chemical	Effect
candles	stearic acid	at 10–20% of total mass, makes candles harder, more opaque, and dripless
Dove bar soap	coconut fatty acids stearic acid	reacted to give detergent sodium cocyl isothionate superfatting—after-feel on skin
shaving cream	sodium stearate	gives small stable bubbles; helps hold water in; lubricates
pump soap	sodium oleate	makes soap a liquid
hand cream	glycerine isopropyl palmitate	humectancy (moisture retention), emolliency (feel on skin)
lipstick	isopropyl myristate	reduces stickiness of castor oil/wax base; prevents drag during application
WD 40	sorbitan oleate	wets metal surfaces
glazing compound	oleic acid	gives fluidity and plasticity to clays
"waterless" hand cleaner	amine salt of oleic acid	emulsifies water and mineral spirits
jet engine lubricant	pelargonic acid ester	fluid at both high and low temperatures; non-volatile
arctic crankcase lubricant	azelaic acid ester	liquid at very low temperatures

Beef tallow is the primary raw material for all of the compounds in Table 1. Other important sources of natural oils include coconuts, soybeans, and kernels from palm and pine trees. All of these raw materials are renewable resources. Some petroleum products are also used as raw materials.

Emery was a Cincinnati-based company for the first 138 years of its existence. In 1978, it was sold to National Distillers (later Quantum Chemical) and operated as a division of that company until 1989 when it was purchased by Henkel Corporation, a large German manufacturer of soaps, detergents, and related products.

Content Review

Fats and Oils: An Introduction

Fatty acids are the building blocks of fats and oils. Fatty acids are long-chain carboxylic acids (organic molecules containing a –COOH group). Most naturally occurring fatty acids have an even number of carbon atoms. Fatty acids with 16 and 18 carbons are very important in the production of many consumer products. The chemical structures of stearic acid, the 18-carbon fatty acid common in fat molecules of beef tallow, and palmitic acid, the 16-carbon fatty acid found in the oil molecules of palm oil, are shown in Figure 1.

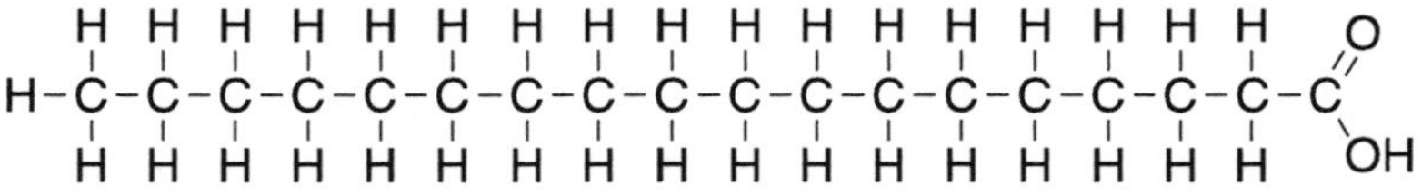

stearic acid
$C_{17}H_{35}COOH$

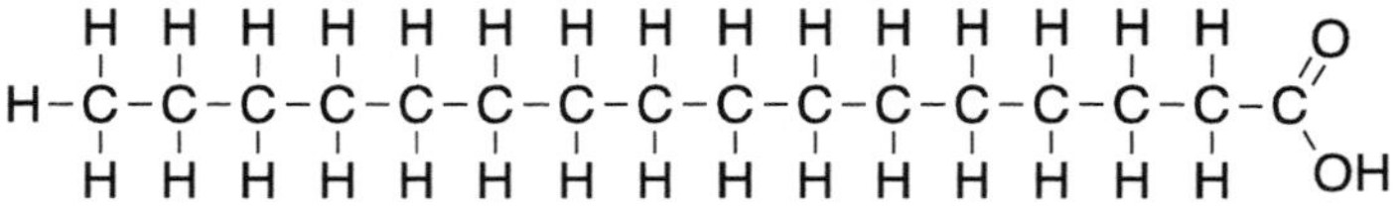

palmitic acid
$C_{15}H_{31}COOH$

Figure 1: The structures of stearic and palmitic acids

The fatty acids shown in Figure 1 both contain only carbon-carbon single bonds (C–C) and are said to be saturated. The length of the carbon chain is important in determining the properties of the fatty acids. For example, the longer the chain, the higher the melting point and the lower the solubility in water and other polar solvents.

If fatty acids contain one or more carbon-carbon double bonds (C=C), they are said to be unsaturated. Monounsaturated fatty acids have only one double bond. Those with two or more are called polyunsaturated fatty acids. Oleic acid is the most common monounsaturated fatty acid. It makes up most of the total fatty acid content of many fats. Its structure is shown in Figure 2.

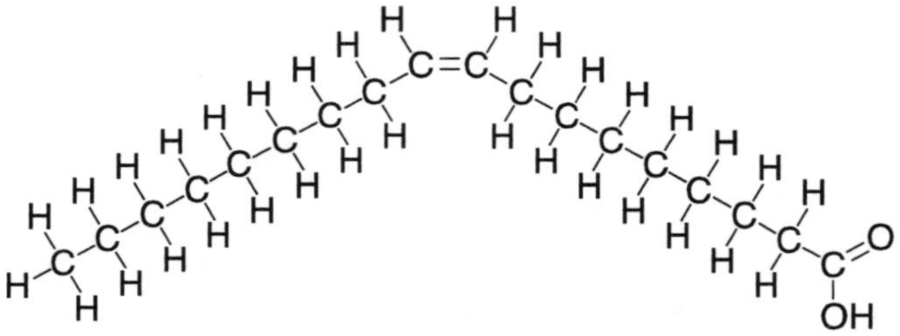

oleic acid
$CH_3(CH_2)_7CH=CH(CH_2)_7COOH$

Figure 2: The structure of oleic acid

Unsaturated acids melt at a lower temperature than their saturated counterparts having the same number of carbon atoms. The commercially important unsaturated fatty acids are liquids at room temperature because the geometry around the C=C double bond prevents efficient packing of the molecules into a solid. As shown in Figure 2, oleic acid is in the cis-orientation (pronounced "sis") about the carbon-carbon double bond. The result of the cis double bond is that the molecules of the unsaturated fatty acid are bent. This bent configuration causes the unsaturated fatty acid to have less interaction between its molecules, resulting in the melting point being lower than that of its saturated fatty acid counterpart.

Fats and oils are chemically classified as triglycerides, complex esters formed from fatty acids and the alcohol, glycerol. An ester is produced when a carboxylic acid reacts with an alcohol in the process called esterification. (The general process is shown in Figure 3a. The R groups, R and R', stand for carbon chains.) The formation of the ester ethyl acetate is shown in Figure 3b.

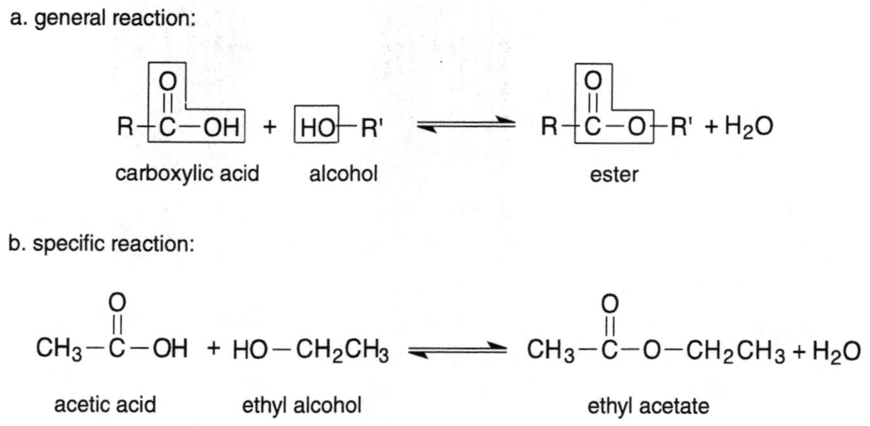

a. general reaction:

$$R-C(=O)-OH + HO-R' \rightleftharpoons R-C(=O)-O-R' + H_2O$$

carboxylic acid   alcohol   ester

b. specific reaction:

$$CH_3-C(=O)-OH + HO-CH_2CH_3 \rightleftharpoons CH_3-C(=O)-O-CH_2CH_3 + H_2O$$

acetic acid   ethyl alcohol   ethyl acetate

Figure 3: The formation of esters. Part a shows the general reaction with the functional groups boxed and labelled. Part b shows a specific example of this reaction in which ethyl acetate is produced.

The forward reaction in Figure 4 is an esterification of glycerol in which one glycerol molecule reacts with three fatty acid molecules to form a triester called a triglyceride. The R groups in commercially important fatty acids contain 6–20 carbon atoms. If the R groups are the same, the molecule is called a simple triglyceride. If the Rs are not all the same, the molecule is called a mixed triglyceride.

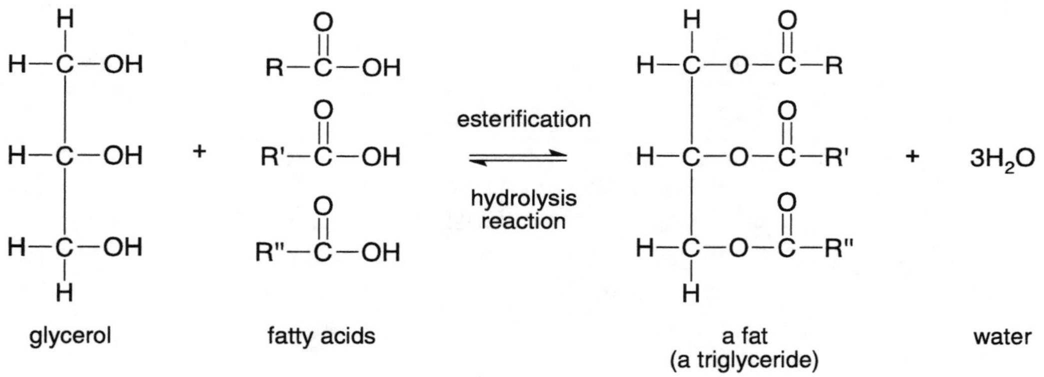

Figure 4: Formation of a triglyceride from glycerol and fatty acids

Fats and Oils as Raw Materials

As discussed in The Emery Group of Henkel Corporation, fats and oils are used by the Emery Group as raw materials. The Emery Group isolates fatty acids and glycerol through different processes and sells these compounds to other manufacturers for use in various products.

Fats and oils are decomposed into their component fatty acids and glycerol by a reaction called hydrolysis, the reverse of the esterification reaction shown in Figure 4. This reaction involves the addition of water under acidic conditions with high temperature (260°C) and high pressure (47.63 atm).

The fatty acids that are liberated during the hydrolysis reaction are water-insoluble and therefore separate from glycerol which is water-soluble and remains in solution. Emery purifies the fatty acids by a combination of distillation and recrystallization from suitable solvents. Glycerol is purified by distillation. Some of the fatty acids and the glycerol are sold, while other fatty acids are converted to other products ("derivatives") and then sold.

Glycerol, like all alcohols, contains the –OH group. The structure of alcohols (ROH) is related to that of water (HOH), and therefore glycerol attracts water molecules; in technical language, it acts as a humectant. It is used in many preparations applied to the skin because it attracts and holds water molecules in the skin, thereby preventing dryness. Due to its relatively non-volatile nature, glycerol's "moisturizing" action lasts a long time.

The kinds of fatty acids obtained from the hydrolysis of triglycerides depend on the nature of the fats or oils hydrolyzed. Typically, animal tallow produces a mixture containing large amounts of stearic, palmitic, and oleic acids, with smaller amounts of other fatty acids. As shown in Table 2, oleic acid melts below room temperature (Room temperature is 25°C) and therefore can be separated from higher melting acids which are solids at this temperature. (The historical way of separating out oleic acid was to press out the liquid oleic acid. Consequently, the grade of stearic acid containing the least oleic acid impurity is still referred to as "triple pressed." Today, however, Henkel uses more modern techniques.)

Table 2: The Melting Points and Molar Masses of Five Common Fatty Acids

Fatty Acid	Melting Point	Molar Mass	Formula
stearic acid	70°C	284.47	$C_{17}H_{35}COOH$
palmitic acid	63°C	256.42	$C_{15}H_{31}COOH$
oleic acid	14°C	282.47	$CH_3(CH_2)_7CH=CH(CH_2)_7COOH$
lauric acid	44°C	200.34	$C_{11}H_{23}COOH$
myristic acid	58°C	228.37	$C_{13}H_{27}COOH$

Various grades of stearic and oleic acids are sold by Emery. A high-purity product is not required for most commercial uses so there is no advantage in incurring the extra expense of isolating a single pure acid from the fatty acid mixture. For fatty acids, physical properties (such as melting point) are more important. In fact, the best-selling "stearic" acid produced by Emery, Emery 132 NF Lily "Stearic" Acid, contains 45.5% stearic, 50% palmitic, and 4.5% unsaturated acids.

Coconut oil is a common vegetable source of fatty acids. The hydrolysis of coconut oil typically yields a mixture of short-chain fatty acids such as lauric and myristic acids. (See Table 2.) These short-chain, saturated fatty acids have lower melting points than longer-chain, saturated fatty acids (e.g., stearic and palmitic acids). Commercial mixtures of fatty acids derived from coconut oil are liquid at or near room temperature because of lower melting points of the individual fatty acid constituents and because, in general, the melting point of a mixture is lower than the melting points of the pure components.

Oilseeds are a plentiful source of vegetable oils. The percent by mass of oils obtained from various kinds of oilseeds is as follows: soybean 18–22%; peanut 46–50%; sunflower 42–60%; coconut 63–70%. The general method for extracting oils from oilseeds is shown in Figure 5. The distribution of fatty acids obtained from various fats and oils is shown in Table 3.

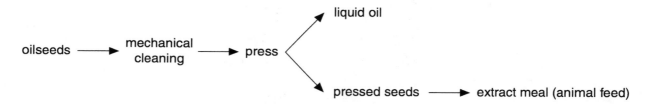

Figure 5: The general method for extracting oils from oilseeds

Table 3: Percent Composition of Fatty Acids in Common Fats and Oils

	Acid	Designation*	Beef Tallow	Soybean	Olive	Whale	Peanut	Sunflower	Corn	Linseed	Coconut
saturated	lauric	$C_{12:0}$	—	0.2	—	0.2	—	—	—	—	45.4
saturated	myristic	$C_{14:0}$	6.3	0.1	trace	9.3	—	—	1.4	—	18.0
saturated	palmitic	$C_{16:0}$	27.4	9.8	6.9	15.6	8.3	5.6	10.2	6.3	10.5
saturated	stearic	$C_{18:0}$	14.1	2.4	2.3	2.8	3.1	2.2	3.0	2.5	2.3
saturated	arachidic	$C_{20:0}$	—	0.9	0.1	—	2.4	0.9	—	0.5	0.4
unsaturated	palmitoleic	$C_{16:1}$	—	0.4	—	14.4	—	—	1.5	—	0.4
unsaturated	oleic	$C_{18:1}$	49.6	28.9	84.4	35.2	56.0	25.1	49.6	19.0	7.5
unsaturated	linoleic	$C_{18:2}$	2.5	50.7	4.6	—	26.0	66.2	34.3	24.1	trace
unsaturated	linolenic	$C_{18:3}$	—	6.5	—	—	—	—	—	47.4	—
unsaturated	other	n/a	—	0.1	—	22.2	4.2	—	—	0.2	—

*The subscripted ratio indicates number of carbons to number of carbon-carbon double bonds.
Source: *Handbook of Biochemistry,* 2nd ed.; Sober, H.A., Ed.; The Chemical Rubber Company: Cleveland, 1970; pp E-20–E-21.

Soap-Making

No one knows who discovered soap, but there are recipes for soap-making which date back to the Phoenicians in 600 B.C. The Egyptians and Romans used oils to clean themselves. Oils dissolved bodily dirt and were removed with fine sand (Egypt) or scraped off with an instrument called a stirgil (Romans). A legend about the origin of soap says that it was discovered outside the city of Rome on Sapo Hill. The poor offered sacrifices to the gods by burning animals on altars erected on the hill. Fat from the animals accumulated on the altars along with ash. When rain fell, the two were washed down into the clay soil. In time, women learned that this clay made washing clothes easier. Thus, legend states that Sapo clay was the origin of soap. This legend has never been verified but the word "sapo" survives in the word for soap in modern European languages—soap, sapone (Italian), savon (French), jabon (Spanish), and seife (German).

By the Middle Ages, centers of soap-making existed in Marseilles, Genoa, Venice, Bari, and Spain, all of which had plentiful supplies of olive oil and barilla (a fleshy plant whose ashes were used to make lye, which today we know provides the base needed for the esterification reaction).

Throughout history, bases used to make soap have been obtained from different sources. One of the earliest bases, potassium carbonate (potash, K_2CO_3), was extracted from wood ashes by treating them with water. Soda ash (Na_2CO_3), mined as the mineral trona, was also used. During the Napoleonic Wars, the British blockaded France and limited their supply of soda ash, threatening soap production. In response to this crisis, Napoleon offered a cash prize to anyone who could provide a substitute. The French chemist Leblanc won the prize when he discovered how to make soda ash from common salt (NaCl), limestone ($CaCO_3$), and ammonia. This not only solved the French problem, but also made soap available to common people everywhere.

The chemistry of making soap involves hydrolizing a triglyceride (fat) with a strong base such as sodium hydroxide (NaOH). The reaction, called saponification, is shown in Figure 6. Soaps are sodium, potassium, or sometimes ammonium salts of fatty acids.

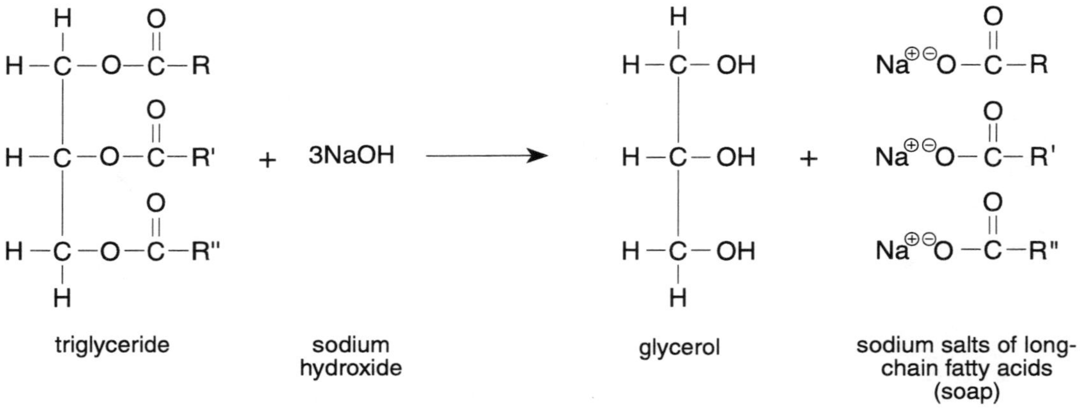

Figure 6: The saponification reaction of a triglyceride

Lubricants

The Emery Group works not only with fats and oils as raw materials, but also with some petroleum products. The Emery Group uses hydrocarbons (molecules containing only carbon and hydrogen) that possess one double bond within the molecule. These particular molecules are called monounsaturated hydrocarbons and are chemically classified as olefins. (Oleic acid is an example of an olefinic fatty acid.) These olefins are used to create polymers. Polymers are long chains of simple molecules called monomers. In this case, the monomer (mono = one; mer = unit) is the olefin and the polymer (poly = many; mer = units) is formed by hooking many of these olefin molecules together.

The specific olefin that Emery uses is called 1-decene, an α-olefin with the double bond located at the end (α) position of the chain. Polymers of α-olefins are called polyalphaolefins (PAO). For example, three molecules can be hooked together to give a trimeric PAO as shown in Figure 7.

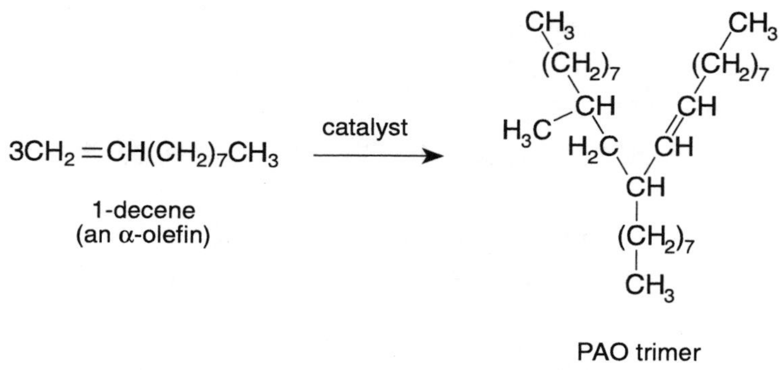

$$3CH_2 = CH(CH_2)_7CH_3 \xrightarrow{\text{catalyst}}$$

1-decene
(an α-olefin)

PAO trimer

Figure 7: The formation of a trimeric PAO

Notice that the decene units are not linked together in a straight chain, but are linked in branched chains. It would be possible under different reaction conditions to link different numbers of 1-decene molecules and to branch the chain differently.

The primary use of PAOs is in synthetic lubricants. Since lubricants are nonreactive compounds, the reactive double bond is hydrogenated, giving a saturated hydrocarbon molecule called a paraffin. This reaction is shown in Figure 8.

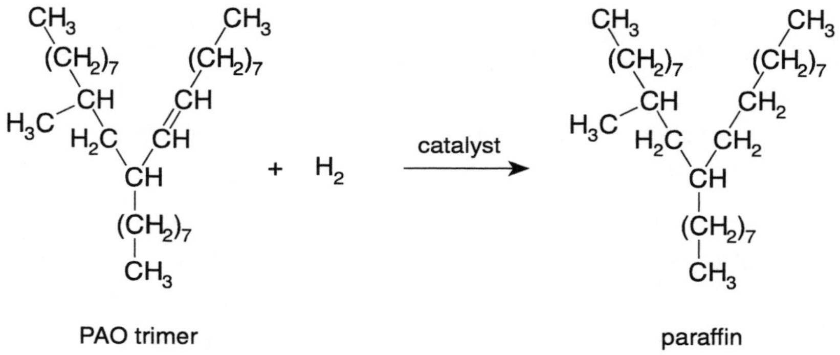

PAO trimer   paraffin

Figure 8: The formation of a paraffin from a trimeric PAO

Synthetic oils are mainly PAOs, esters, polyglycols, and silicones. The latter two are not discussed here, since they are not manufactured by Emery. The advantage of PAO synthetic base stocks (materials used to blend synthetic lubricants) is that their hydrocarbon composition is similar to that of naturally occurring petroleum-based oils.

Lubricants are very important in a society which relies heavily on machinery. The heavier fractions obtained in the distillation of petroleum are sometimes used as lubricants; however, the range of properties such as freezing point and ability to flow are restricted to those compounds that occur naturally in petroleum deposits. Compounds that are made synthetically can be designed to exhibit desirable lubricant properties. The synthetics can be blended with natural petroleum lubricants, with other synthetics, or used alone. Emery Group of Henkel Corporation produces a variety of synthetic lubricants.

Lubricants (commonly called oil, grease, etc.) are used by our society in machinery to reduce friction, prolong the useful lifetime, and as sealants. Friction produces heat and wear and is undesirable in operating machinery. Liquid lubricants reduce friction by coating metal to prevent direct contact between metal parts. Moreover, oil, a widely used lubricant, removes heat from automobile engines and transfers it to the cooling system. Lubricants also keep dirt and metal particles which wear off engine parts suspended until they reach the oil filter, where they are trapped. Water is also carried away by the engine oil. Additives are usually put into oil to react with corrosive compounds that form when the engine runs and to prevent corrosion. Oil improves fuel economy (up to 5%) by helping to seal engine valves, where the fuel/air mixture is ignited. A pressure increase occurs during ignition and drives the piston. This pressure is maximized if no gas can escape.

Eventually motor oil becomes contaminated with by-products of fuel combustion, dirt, and sludge. It may also begin to break down chemically as a result of high engine temperatures. As a result, oil needs to be changed periodically.

As stated previously, an important lubricant property is the ability to coat moving parts and to flow through the engine. The resistance of a fluid to flow is called its viscosity. In general, the viscosity of fluids decreases as the temperature increases. Since operating temperatures for machinery can vary from quite cold when started to very hot after some running time, a lubricant designed for minimum viscosity change with temperature is desirable. Lubricants of low viscosity circulate in the engine more easily and coat parts effectively at cold temperatures. High-viscosity lubricants protect engine parts better and make engines run more quietly. It would be ideal for motor oils to have both kinds of viscosity characteristics. Different motor oils can be "blended" to achieve this combination of characteristics.

Viscosity properties are specified by Society of Automotive Engineers (SAE) numbers. The higher the number, the higher the viscosity. Single-grade oils have one number such as SAE30. Blended oils have two numbers, such as SAE10W40. (The W stands for winter.) The first number is the viscosity at −18°C (−0.4°F); the second is the viscosity at 99°C (210.2°F). SAE10W40 and Emery Emgard E2811 show less variation of flow time with temperature than non-blended SAE30.

Petroleum-based lubricating oils are composed mainly of high-molar-mass hydrocarbons obtained from the distillation of petroleum. These oils contain molecules with 17 or more carbons and boiling points above 300°C. Also present in the mixtures are paraffinic waxes; unsaturated compounds; and aromatic compounds, such as naphthalene; all of which adversely affect viscosity.

In contrast to petroleum-based lubricants, synthetic lubricants have excellent viscosity/temperature properties. In cold weather, engines that contain synthetic oil usually start more easily without "starter groan" and engine warm-up takes place rapidly. This is because the engine oil is entirely fluid. In contrast, the thick oils and waxes in petroleum oil require a longer warm-up time to become fluid in the engine. Synthetic motor oils also have better resistance to oxidation and are good solvents for many of the additives dissolved in modern oils. They are a natural detergent and therefore act as scavenging agents for dirt and fuel deposits, carrying them to the oil filter.

Using the Activities in the Classroom

The activities in this module help students become aware of the importance of oleochemistry and its relationship to the oleochemical industry.

Pedagogical Strategies

The activities in this module range from simple, for those with little background or time, to those that are more complex, for those with more science background and/or time. It is important that you read through each activity, try it, and then adjust it according to the needs of the learners.

Even if soap or candles are not made, lessons can be centered around them by using commercially prepared substances. Since all students use soap/detergents at home, samples can be obtained, eliminating the need to buy all materials. Interesting discoveries are often made in this way.

Individual and Group Projects

Relating the activities and substances to advertising can be a great analytical lesson. Ads from magazines or videotaped commercials can be viewed and analyzed and the product tested to see if it meets the advertised claims.

Creating wrappers or labels for products made in the activities is another way to relate consumerism to the lesson. Students find this a change of pace and a chance to use their creativity and artistic talents.

Surveys can be taken and comparisons made of different brands of soap or detergent. Emphasize the collection and use of data. Discuss how manufacturers use this type of data.

Cross-Curricular Integration

Relate the history of soaps, candles, or lubricants to American or ancient history. Without getting into minute detail, an appreciation of the progress humans have made can become apparent.

Science-Technology-Society (S-T-S)

Science-Technology-Society issues can be integrated with the oleochemistry module, particularly with the activities involving the soap industry. Among many other publications, *The Science Teacher* and the Science Education Council of Ohio (SECO) newsletter often include articles that are relevant to S-T-S.

Annotated List of Activities and Demonstrations

To aid you in choosing activities for your classroom, we have included an annotated list of activities and demonstrations. This listing includes information about the grade level that can benefit most from an activity and a brief description of each activity. A Curriculum Placement Guide follows this list.

1. **Esters** (upper elementary to high school)
   Students produce esters from the appropriate alcohol and carboxylic acid and try to identify the ester by its odor.

2. **Making Candles** (upper elementary to high school)
   Students make regular and dripless candles and compare these candles.

3. **Candle Investigations** (upper elementary to high school)
   Students perform a variety of tests on candles. These tests include studying a burning candle and identifying combustion products.

4. **Making Cleansing Cream** (upper elementary to high school)
   Create your own cleansing cream using an emulsion of stearic acid, paraffin wax, mineral oil, borax, and water.

5. **Preparation and Comparison of Four Soaps** (upper elementary to high school)
   Students make their own soaps using lard, stearic acid, oleic acid, coconut fatty acid, and sodium or potassium hydroxide. These soaps are then tested for lathering ability, behavior in hard water, and excess alkali.

6. **Surface Tension** (elementary to high school)
   Students investigate surface tension through a series of activities and also discover how soaps and detergents affect surface tension.

7. **Blowing Bubbles** (elementary to high school)
   Why do bubbles form? Why are they spherical? Why are they different colors? Students blow bubbles using a homemade bubble solution and compare them to commercially prepared bubble solutions.

8. **Food Colors in Milk** (elementary to high school)
   Students create and observe a swirling mixture of colors caused by the interaction of the fat in milk and liquid dishwashing detergent.

9. **Emulsifying Peanut or Vegetable Oil** (upper elementary to high school)
   Can oil and water mix? In this activity, oil and water mix when detergent is added.

10. **Properties of Lubricants** (middle to high school)
    Students investigate the properties of viscosity and density of various types of motor oils.

11. **Make-It-Yourself Slime** (elementary to high school)
    Students make and study the properties of a polymer similar to the familiar toy Slime®.

Topics

Activities	Nature of Matter	Science-Technology-Society	Scientific Method	Health	Mass, Volume, and Density	Chemical Reactivity	Laboratory Techniques	Organic Chemistry	Polymers	Acid-Base
1 Esters	•	•				•	•	•		
2 Making Candles	•	•	•			•	•	•		•
3 Candle Investigations	•	•	•		•	•	•	•		
4 Making Cleansing Cream	•	•	•	•	•	•	•	•		
5 Preparation and Comparison of Four Soaps	•	•	•	•		•	•	•		
6 Surface Tension	•	•	•				•			
7 Blowing Bubbles	•		•							
8 Food Colors in Milk	•	•	•	•		•	•			
9 Emulsifying Peanut or Vegetable Oil	•	•	•	•	•	•	•	•		
10 Properties of Lubricants	•	•	•		•		•			
11 Make-It-Yourself Slime	•	•	•		•	•			•	

Activities and Demonstrations

1. Esters 21

2. Making Candles 27

3. Candle Investigations 33

4. Making Cleansing Cream 41

5. Preparation and Comparison of Four Soaps 47

6. Surface Tension 57

7. Blowing Bubbles 65

8. Food Colors in Milk 71

9. Emulsifying Peanut or Vegetable Oil 77

10. Properties of Lubricants 83

11. Make-It-Yourself Slime 91

Esters

1

What makes a banana taste like a banana? Many natural and artificial flavorings belong to a class of compounds called esters. Esters are produced by a chemical process called esterification, and in this activity, students have the chance to prepare and examine several synthetic flavorings that are esters.

Recommended Grade Level .... **Part 1: 4–8, Part 2: 7–12**
Group Size .... **1–4 students**
Time for Preparation .... **30 minutes**
Time for Procedure: .... **Part 1: 25 minutes (+ 1 hour for heating)**
Part 2: 45 minutes

Materials

Opening Strategy
Per Student
- food flavorings and/or extracts

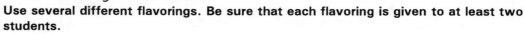
Use several different flavorings. Be sure that each flavoring is given to at least two students.

- cotton ball
- small plastic zipper-type bag or film canister
- (optional) balloon

Procedure, Part 1
Per Group
- 0.2 g (a large pinch) Dowex® 50x2-100 cation exchange resin
- medium-sized test tube (e.g., 13-mm x 100-mm or 16-mm x 150-mm)
- 2–3 small boiling stones
- a sand bath made from the following:
    - fine, clean sand (e.g., fine play sand)
    - 150-mL beaker or similar glass container
- hot plate
- alcohol or metal thermometer that reads at least as high as 150°C
- 50-mL beaker
- 0.8 g potassium carbonate (K_2CO_3)
- 1 or more of the alcohol/carboxylic acid pairs shown in Table 1
- goggles

Procedure, Part 2 (Optional)
Per Group
- 3 or more small test tubes (e.g., 12-mm x 75-mm)
- 400-mL beaker
- 3 or more 125-mL Erlenmeyer flasks
- hot plate or Bunsen burner, ringstand, and wire gauze
- 1 or more of the alcohol/carboxylic acid pairs shown in Table 1

- test tube holder or pair of tongs
- goggles

Per Class
- 100 mL concentrated sulfuric acid (18 M H_2SO_4) in a glass dropper bottle
- plastic gloves

Variation
- several balloons
- food flavorings
- string

Table 1: Alcohol/Carboxylic Acid Pairs and Resulting Esters

Alcohol	Carboxylic Acid	Ester	Odor of Ester
0.5 mL isoamyl (isopentyl) alcohol	1.5 mL ethanoic (acetic) acid	isoamyl acetate	banana
0.5 mL octanol	1.5 mL ethanoic (acetic) acid	octyl acetate	bitter orange (citrus, orange)
0.5 mL isobutanol	0.5 mL formic acid	isobutyl formate	raspberry
1.0 mL methanol	0.5 mL salicylic acid	methyl salicylate	oil of wintergreen
0.5 mL n-propanol	1.5 mL ethanoic (acetic) acid	propyl acetate	pear

Resources

Most of the chemicals for this activity can be purchased from Flinn Scientific, P.O. Box 219, Batavia, IL 60510-0219, 800/452-1261.

- potassium carbonate—catalog # P0038 for 500 g
- sulfuric acid (18 M)—catalog # S0228 for 100 mL
- methanol—catalog # M0054 for 500 mL
- ethanol—catalog # E0007 for 500 mL
- isobutanol—catalog # I0017 for 500 mL
- isoamyl alcohol—catalog # I0031 for 100 mL
- formic acid—catalog # F0044 for 100 mL
- ethanoic acid (acetic acid)—catalog # A0177 for 100 mL
- salicylic acid—catalog # S0001 for 100 g
- octanol—catalog # Q0018 for 100 mL
- n-propanol—catalog # P0228 for 100 mL

Dowex 50x2-100 cation exchange resin can be purchased from Aldrich Chemical Company, 1001 West St. Paul Ave., Milwaukee, WI 53233, 800/558-9160.

- Dowex 50x2-100 resin—catalog # 21,744-1 for 100 g

Safety and Disposal

Goggles should be worn when performing this activity. The concentrated sulfuric acid (18 M H_2SO_4) is very corrosive and can cause severe chemical burns if it comes in contact with the skin or eyes. Handle with extreme care. The 18 M H_2SO_4 should be dispensed by the instructor. Wear gloves to protect your hands while dispensing the 18 M H_2SO_4. If contact occurs, flush the affected area with water for at least 15 minutes. If contact involves the eyes, seek medical attention immediately while continuing to flush the area with water.

Methanol ("wood alcohol") is very toxic if ingested and can be absorbed through the skin. If contact occurs, rinse the affected area with water. Methanol is also highly flammable and should be kept away from open flames. Methanol should be dispensed by the instructor. Wear gloves to protect your hands while dispensing the alcohol.

The water should be heated and the flame turned off before the test tubes are placed into the water. Alcohols are flammable and should be kept away from the flame or hot plate while in use.

Do not let students smell their esters by holding the flasks under their noses. Instead, they should use the wafting procedure described in Employing Appropriate Safety Procedures.

In large amounts, esters, including those listed in Table 1, can be toxic. (Only very small amounts of esters are present in foods.) In addition, the crude esters synthesized in this activity may contain significant amounts of toxic impurities. Students should never be allowed to taste products that have been made in the laboratory or in lab glassware.

Getting Ready

Prepare the sand baths by half-filling a 150-mL beaker with sand and warming it to 120°C using a hot plate.

Opening Strategy

Introduce the students to esters by placing a cotton ball with 2–3 drops of each flavoring in a separate small plastic bag or film canister. Number each bag and keep a key of which flavor extract is in each bag. Try to use as many flavoring extracts as possible and make at least two of each scent. Each student should receive a numbered plastic bag. Have the students go around the classroom and try to find other students with the same scent as they have. Once they have found another student with the same scent, have them stay together as a group until each student is in a group. Then explain to students that the different scents are chemicals called esters and are used in food flavorings for cooking and baking.

Another idea would be to put a few drops of vanilla extract into a balloon. Inflate the balloon and tie the end. Pass the balloon around the class to see if the students can identify the odor. Introduce the idea that odors are chemicals. Many chemicals (including vanillin) that have strong odors belong to a class of chemicals called esters. In this activity, students will make esters that may have recognizable odors.

Procedure

Part 1: Using Dowex Beads

1. Place about 0.2 g (a large pinch) Dowex 50x2-100 beads into a test tube.

2. Add the appropriate amounts of the desired alcohol and the corresponding carboxylic acid from Table 1 to the beads. (Twenty drops equals approximately 1 mL.)

 Never smell unknown materials by holding them directly under your nose. (Salicylic acid has no odor, and acetic acid is a concentrated form of vinegar with a strong odor.)

3. Carefully smell the contents of the test tube by waving your hand across the mouth of the test tube to push the vapor toward your nose. Describe the odor of the starting reagents and record the observation.

4. Add two or three small boiling stones to the test tube to help prevent the contents of the test tube from frothing during the heating in Step 5.

5. Stand the test tubes in a sand bath that has been warmed to 120°C. Allow the test tube to heat for about 1 hour.

6. After 1 hour of heating, pour the contents of the test tube into a 50-mL beaker containing 0.8 g of potassium carbonate (K_2CO_3).

7. Smell the contents of the beaker (by wafting) and record the odor of the ester that has been produced. Rinse the contents of the beaker down the drain with water.

Part 2: Using Concentrated Sulfuric Acid (Optional)

 This procedure is NOT recommended for the elementary classroom due to the use of concentrated sulfuric acid (18 M H_2SO_4). See Safety and Disposal.

1. Add about 200 mL water to the 400-mL beaker. Heat the water until it boils and then turn off the hot plate or burner.

2. Add 10 drops (0.5 mL) of one of the alcohols from Table 1 to a clean, dry test tube.

3. Add the appropriate amount of the carboxylic acid listed next to the alcohol in Table 1.

 The instructor should dispense the sulfuric acid in the next step. If contact occurs, rinse thoroughly with water for 15 minutes. See Safety and Disposal.

4. Add two drops of the concentrated sulfuric acid.

5. Use a test tube holder or pair of tongs to place the test tube in the beaker of near-boiling water. Let stand in the hot-water bath for 5 minutes.

6. Add water to the 125-mL Erlenmeyer flask until it is about ⅓ full. Pour the contents of the test tube from Step 5 into the flask and swirl the flask.

 Never smell unknown materials by holding them directly under your nose. Use the wafting procedure described in Employing Appropriate Safety Procedures. Use EXTREME caution wafting the solution that still contains sulfuric acid.

7. Carefully smell the ester by waving your hand across the mouth of the flask to push the vapor toward your nose. Describe the odor of the sample and record the observation. Rinse the contents of the flask down the drain with water.

8. (optional) Repeat Steps 2–7 for another pair of alcohols and acids from Table 1.

Variation

- Provide some commercial esters (or food flavorings) for the students to smell by placing a few drops of each into a separate balloon. Inflate it and tie the end. Pass the balloons around the class to see if students can identify the odor. Have them compare these flavorings with the compounds formed in the experiment. Some students might recognize the odors, but not be able to identify the exact food flavoring. Make a chart on the blackboard and pool the class results. Reiterate the concept that these odors are chemicals and explain that many chemicals that have strong odors belong to a class of chemicals called esters.

Discussion

- Discuss how the Dowex resin or sulfuric acid functions in the reactions.
  They both act as catalysts to cause reactions to proceed.

- Ask students why using a natural flavoring (such as chocolate) would sometimes be preferable to using an artificial flavoring.
  Some artificial flavorings can be produced to taste just like the natural flavors such as oil of wintergreen. Other natural flavorings, such as chocolate, are such a complex mixture of chemicals that scientists have yet to make an artificial flavor that tastes just like the natural one.

Explanation

An ester is formed when a carboxylic acid reacts with an alcohol in a process known as esterification. During esterification the −OH group from the acid combines with a −H from the alcohol, forming H_2O. This reaction typically requires a catalyst to speed it. For decades, concentrated sulfuric acid (18 M H_2SO_4) has been used as the catalyst (as in the Procedure, Part 2). Its dehydrating capability makes it effective for this purpose. However, for the same reason, it is very dangerous to use. It can cause severe chemical burns that result from the dehydration of the proteins in your skin. The procedure suggested in Part 1 uses a relatively new and safe acidic material called a cation exchange resin; its trade name is Dowex 50x2-100, and it is manufactured by the Dow Chemical Company. The Dowex resin reacts just as the concentrated sulfuric acid does by scavenging the water produced by the esterification reaction and drives the reaction toward producing an ester. Sample equations for the esterification process are shown in Figure 1.

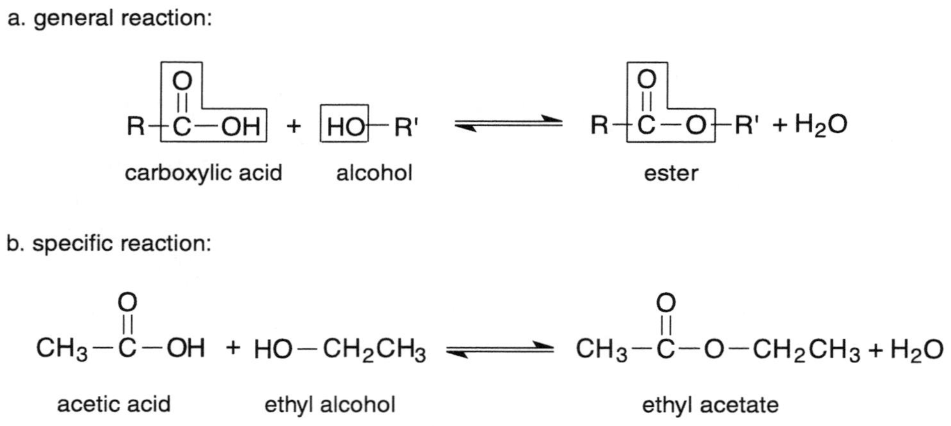

a. general reaction:

$$R-\overset{\overset{\displaystyle O}{\|}}{C}-OH \quad + \quad HO-R' \quad \rightleftharpoons \quad R-\overset{\overset{\displaystyle O}{\|}}{C}-O-R' \quad +H_2O$$

carboxylic acid   alcohol   ester

b. specific reaction:

$$CH_3-\overset{\overset{\displaystyle O}{\|}}{C}-OH \quad + \quad HO-CH_2CH_3 \quad \rightleftharpoons \quad CH_3-\overset{\overset{\displaystyle O}{\|}}{C}-O-CH_2CH_3 + H_2O$$

acetic acid   ethyl alcohol   ethyl acetate

Figure 1: The reaction of a carboxylic acid and an alcohol to form an ester

When low-molecular-weight carboxylic acids are esterified, the resulting esters are typically colorless liquids with fruity odors. These synthetic esters are used in the food industry as flavorings. In many cases, the esters produced in the laboratory are the same molecules that give fruits their characteristic flavors. For example, isoamyl acetate, the chemical that gives bananas their characteristic flavor, can be made in the lab by reacting isoamyl alcohol with acetic acid. Other synthetic esters have no natural counterparts. However, they do have fruity flavors that can be used in foods.

Key Science Concepts

- catalysts
- esters

Cross-Curricular Integration

Home, Safety, and Career
Have students use natural and synthetic flavorings in recipes and assess both types of flavorings based on factors such as cost, ease of use, storage life, and quality of taste.

Social Studies
Discuss the impact of artificial flavors and sweeteners on the natural flavorings market. Students could also research other synthetics such as synthetic rubber, nylon, and dyes, and the effect their production has on the markets for their natural counterparts.

Reference

An activity dealing with the synthesis of flavors also appears in the *Dirt Alert* and *Science Fare* modules of the *Science in Our World* series.

Making Candles

Have you ever wondered why some candles drip while others don't? The difference results from the composition of the candles. Stearic acid, one of the fatty acids produced by Henkel Corporation, Emery Division, is an important component of dripless candles. In this activity, students make candles with and without stearic acid and observe differences in the way they burn.

Recommended Grade Level 4–12
Group Size .... 1–4 students
Time for Preparation .... none
Time for Procedure .... 40–50 minutes (+ 3–4 hours for candles to cure)

Materials

Opening Strategy
Per Class
- paraffin wax candle
- dripless candle made with stearic acid
- matches

Procedure, Parts 1 and 2
Per Candle
- 50 g paraffin wax
- metal weight (e.g., small hexnut or washer)
- orange juice can, 50-mL beaker, or other mold
- 1 of the following wicks:
    - size 1B wick (for candle diameter under 2 in)
    - size 2B wick (for candle diameter 2–3½ in)
    - wick with wire in it (no hexnut/washer needed)
- scissors to cut wicks
- balance
- hot plate
- 25–100-mL graduated cylinder
- pen or pencil (to suspend wick)
- small wooden stick or toothpick
- 250-mL or 500-mL beaker to melt wax
- plastic spoon or scoop
- watch glass or wet cloth
- (optional) small pieces or shavings of a crayon, preferably Crayola®
- (optional) ice-water bath or access to a refrigerator
- (optional) hot-water bath
- goggles

Procedure, Part 2 Only
- 5–15 g Emersol 132 NF Lily Stearic Acid

Procedure, Part 3
Per Class
- matches
- paraffin candle
- dripless candle made with stearic acid

Resources

Paraffin wax and stearic acid can be purchased from a chemical supply company such as Flinn Scientific, P.O. Box 219, Batavia, IL 60510-0219, 800/452-1261.

- paraffin wax—catalog # P0003 for 500 g
- stearic acid—catalog # S0335 for 100 g

Stearic acid can also be purchased from Henkel Corporation, Emery Group, Attn: Jon Heimann, 4900 Este Avenue, Cincinnati, OH 45232, 513/482-4201.

Candle wicks can be purchased at craft stores.

Safety and Disposal

Goggles should be worn when performing this activity.

Use care when handling hot wax as it can cause burns and damage clothing. Wax that sets into clothing can usually be removed by ironing over the affected area with a paper towel between the iron and the fabric.

Proper fire safety should be exercised such as working on a flame-resistant surface and removing unnecessary flammable materials from the area. Long-haired people should tie hair back when working near a flame.

Paraffin wax is flammable. The wax should not be heated above 95°C (203°F) as it may ignite. If a Bunsen burner is used, melt the paraffin wax in a hot-water bath. Do not leave the paraffin unattended while heating it. If the paraffin wax ignites, cover the beaker with a watch glass or wet cloth to shut off the air supply to the fire.

Opening Strategy

Burn a paraffin wax candle and a dripless candle for the students. Ask them to observe the two candles and describe any differences that they observe between the candles. Explain that one is made of paraffin wax and the other is made of paraffin and stearic acid. Challenge students to determine the reason stearic acid is sometimes added to paraffin to make candles.

Procedure

Part 1: Preparing Paraffin Wax Candles

1. Measure the volume of the candle mold by filling the mold with water and pouring the water into a graduated cylinder. To determine the approximate mass of paraffin needed to make the candle, multiply the volume of the mold by 0.90 g/mL (the density of paraffin).

2. Weigh out the amount of paraffin wax determined in Step 1 and place the wax in a 250-mL or 500-mL beaker.

3. (optional) Add several small pieces or shavings of a crayon to the paraffin to make a colored candle.

4. Cut a piece of wick the length of the mold plus about 10 cm (about 4 in).

5. Tie a metal weight on one end of the wick and wind the other end around the middle of a pen or pencil, leaving just enough wick to reach from the bottom to the top of the mold without sagging.

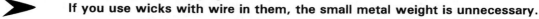 **If you use wicks with wire in them, the small metal weight is unnecessary.**

6. Rest the pen or pencil on the rim of the mold so that the metal weight tied to the wick just touches the bottom of the container.

 Paraffin is flammable and should not be heated with an open flame in the following steps. If at any point the paraffin ignites, extinguish the fire by covering the beaker with a watch glass or wet cloth to shut off the air supply to the flame.

7. Place the beaker on the hot plate over medium heat to melt the paraffin.

8. Continue to heat the paraffin until all of it liquefies, and then carefully pour the liquid paraffin into the prepared mold.

> **If you have extra paraffin remaining after filling the candle mold, do not discard it. You will need the extra paraffin for Step 10.**

9. After about 1½ hours, use a small wooden stick or toothpick to poke a few small holes in the wax on top of the candle near the wick.

10. Allow the candle to sit undisturbed for 1½–2½ hours more to cure.

> **The small holes allow heat from inside the candle to escape; the wax on the outside cools and hardens before the wax on the inside. The wax inside pulls away from the rigid outside wax as it contracts, leaving a cavity inside.**

11. When the candle is cured, fill the cavity in the center of the candle with additional liquid paraffin from Step 8 (reheated if needed).

12. When the newer paraffin is cured, remove the candle from the mold. (Putting the candle and mold in an ice bath or refrigerator may help you to remove the candle from the mold more easily. If, after cooling the candle, you still cannot remove it from the mold, try briefly placing the mold in boiling water until the outer layer of the wax begins to melt. Do not heat the wax above 95°C (205°F) or leave the paraffin unattended while heating it. See Safety and Disposal.)

Part 2: Preparing Dripless Candles

Repeat Part 1 except in Step 2, add 5–15 g stearic acid for every 50 g paraffin used and stir. You may wish to have each group add different proportions of stearic acid to the paraffin to determine an optimum amount of stearic acid for making the dripless candle.

Part 3: Investigations

1. Study an unlit paraffin candle and a candle made with paraffin and stearic acid. What obvious physical differences are there?

2. Light a paraffin candle and a candle made with paraffin and stearic acid. Observe how they burn.

   • Is one candle producing more smoke? (The candles should smoke equally.)

   • Is one candle dripping more? (The stearic acid and paraffin candle should not drip and the paraffin only candle should drip.)

Explanation

Prior to the early 19th century, candles were made from tallow (fat). These candles smoked and dripped excessively. Paraffin was first prepared in 1850. It is a mixture of saturated hydrocarbons (hydrogen- and carbon-containing compounds with the general formula C_nH_{2n+2}) with molecular formulas that range from $C_{18}H_{38}$ to $C_{32}H_{66}$. While used for a variety of applications, paraffin is perhaps best known for its use in making candles. When burned, paraffin emits more light per unit of weight than tallow. However, like tallow, paraffin has a softening point somewhat below its melting point and therefore has a tendency to drip. Stearic acid ($C_{17}H_{35}COOH$) has a higher melting point than paraffin. When stearic acid is added to paraffin, the softening point of the mixture is higher, making the candles dripless. Stearic acid also makes candles opaque.

When a candle is lit, the wax (paraffin and, in dripless candles, stearic acid) in the wick melts due to the heat of the match. Additional wax in the candle itself melts from the heat of the candle flame. This liquid wax is drawn up the wick by capillary action and vaporizes. The vapor burns in oxygen present in the atmosphere.

The candle's flame consists of three regions. (See Figure 1.) Very close to the candle wick is a nonluminous region that contains vaporized paraffin and stearic acid. In the midsection of the flame, partial combustion of the wax occurs, producing carbon (C) and water (H_2O). In the outermost part of the flame, complete oxidation of the carbon to carbon dioxide (CO_2) occurs.

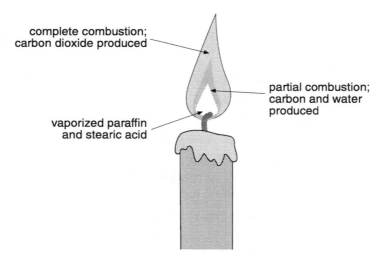

Figure 1: A candle flame consists of three regions.

The net equations for the burning of paraffin and stearic acid are shown in Figure 2. Paraffin is a complex mixture of hydrocarbon chains varying in length from 18 to 32 carbons. The number of carbons is represented by "n" in the equation.

$$2 C_n H_{(2n+2)} \text{ (g)} \ + \ (3n+1) \ O_2 \text{ (g)} \longrightarrow 2n \ CO_2 \text{ (g)} \ + \ (2n+2) \ H_2O \text{ (g)}$$

| paraffin | oxygen | carbon dioxide | water |

$$C_{17}H_{35}CO_2H \text{ (g)} \ + \ 26 \ O_2 \longrightarrow 18 \ CO_2 \text{ (g)} \ + \ 18 \ H_2O \text{ (g)}$$

| stearic acid | oxygen | carbon dioxide | water |

Figure 2: The net equations for the burning of paraffin and stearic acid

Explanations for the Investigations in Part 3

1. **Comparing physical properties of paraffin candle and paraffin and stearic acid candle:** One difference between the two types of candles is that the candle made with paraffin and stearic acid is opaque, while the candle made with only paraffin is translucent.

2. **Comparing burning of paraffin candle and paraffin and stearic acid candle:** The candle made with paraffin and stearic acid should drip noticeably less than the candle made with only paraffin because stearic acid raises the softening point of the wax.

Key Science Concepts

- combustion
- heat production
- mixtures

Cross-Curricular Integration

Art
Have students make sand-cast or other artistic candles.

Language Arts
Have students develop advertisements for their homemade candles.

Social Studies
Study the methods pioneers used to make candles.

References

Hans Jurgen Press. *Simple Science Experiments;* Discovery Toys: USA, 1967.

"Investigating a Burning Candle;" *Fun with Chemistry: A Guidebook of K–12 Activities;* Sarquis, M., Sarquis, J., Eds.; Institute for Chemical Education: Madison, WI, 1992; Vol. 2, pp 339–346.

Wyatt, C., Colerain High School, Cincinnati, OH, personal communication.

Candle Investigations

What really happens when a candle burns? In this activity, students carry out a number of investigations to discover the answer to this question.

> **Recommended Grade Level** .... **7–12 as an activity**
> **4–6 as a demonstration**
> **Group Size** .... **1–4 students**
> **Time for Preparation** .... **30 minutes**
> **Time for Procedure** .... **50 minutes**

Materials

Opening Strategy

- 2 candles
- candle holder
- matches

Procedure

The following materials are needed for 10 separate investigations. Amounts are intended for each investigation to be done once.

Per Class
- balance
- matches
- 10-cm x 10-cm aluminum foil square
- test tube holder or spring-type clothespin
- wire kitchen strainer
- bowl
  2 wide-mouthed glass bottles or jars of different sizes, at least 3 cm taller than candle
- cobalt chloride test paper purchased or made from the following:
  - 10 g cobalt chloride hexahydrate ($CoCl_2 \cdot 6H_2O$)
  - 150-mL beaker
  - filter paper, paper towels, or coffee filter
- ceramic saucer
- 1 of the following:
  - limewater
  - 1.4 g calcium hydroxide, $Ca(OH)_2$, and a container holding 1 L water
- 2 jars with lids
- long matches
- new drinking straws
- large coffee can
- small soup can
- watch glass or wet cloth
- glass stirring rod

- thermometer
- punch can opener
- ring stand
- 2 ring clamps
- wire gauze
- 250-mL graduated cylinder or 1-cup measure
- a variety of candles including the following:
    - paraffin candle
    - dripless candle made with stearic acid
    - several candles of different diameters
    - short candle
    - 2 candles with large diameters
    - up to 7 additional candles of any type

 Fewer candles are needed if investigations are not being done simultaneously.

Resources

Calcium hydroxide, limewater solution, cobalt chloride, and cobalt chloride test papers can be purchased from a chemical supply company such as Flinn Scientific, P.O. Box 219, Batavia, IL 60510-0219, 800/452-1261.

- calcium hydroxide—catalog # C0197 for 100 g
- limewater solution—catalog # L0021 for 500 mL
- cobalt chloride hexahydrate—catalog # C0225 for 25 g
- cobalt chloride test papers—catalog # AP7901 for 12 vials

Safety and Disposal

Use care when handling hot wax as it can cause burns and damage clothing. Wax that sets into clothing can usually be removed by ironing over the affected area with a paper towel between the iron and the fabric.

Proper fire safety should be exercised such as working on a flame-resistant surface and removing unnecessary flammable materials from the area. Long-haired people should tie hair back when working near a flame. Have a watch glass or wet cloth at hand to extinguish flames if the paraffin ignites.

Cobalt chloride ($CoCl_2$) is harmful if taken internally. It is also a possible skin irritant. Remind students not to taste it and to wash well if skin contact occurs. Unused solution may be stored for future use.

Getting Ready

1. If test paper is not purchased, prepare the cobalt chloride test paper for Step 7 as follows:

    a. Dissolve 10 g cobalt chloride hexahydrate ($CoCl_2 \cdot 6H_2O$) in 100 mL water in a 150-mL beaker.

    b. Cut coffee filters, paper towels, or filter paper into strips 3–5 inches long.

c. Dip the strips briefly in the cobalt chloride solution and allow them to dry. If they do not turn from pink to blue within 24 hours, place them in a barely-warm oven, 225°F (107°C) for 5 minutes or until they turn blue.

d. Place the strips in a jar and seal tightly to prevent moisture from turning the strips pink. (If the strips do turn pink, heat them again.)

2. If limewater is not purchased, prepare a limewater solution for Step 9 by adding enough calcium hydroxide, $Ca(OH)_2$, to 1 L water to leave a visible amount of undissolved calcium hydroxide in the container. Shake and stir intermittently for 5–10 minutes. Allow the mixture to settle overnight. Do not mix again. Decant off clear supernatant liquid as needed.

Opening Strategy

Put one candle in a candle holder, set it on a table, and light it. Light another candle and hold it in your hand. Gently blow out the candle in the candle holder. Quickly pass the flame of the candle you are holding through the white smoke coming from the extinguished candle. (Be careful not to drip hot wax on your hand.) The candle that had been extinguished relights. Ask the students to explain how the candle was relit and how a candle burns.

Procedure

Each step is an independent investigation. You can demonstrate these investigations to the class, challenging them with the questions provided. Alternatively, you may wish to assign the investigations to groups. Once the groups have conducted their investigations, they can demonstrate them to the class.

1. Light several paraffin candles of different diameters and watch them burn. What is consumed as the candle burns? Do candles of different diameters decrease in height at the same rate? Note the pool of liquid at the base of the wick. Tip the candle to allow the liquid to drip and solidify on a cool surface. Ask, "What does the appearance of the resolidified liquid suggest about its identity?"

2. Blow out a candle. Quickly light a match and move its flame to the top of the white smoke rising from the candle. (See Figure 1.) The candle will relight with the flame traveling down through the smoke to the wick. (This investigation may need to be repeated a few times so that everyone clearly sees what happens.) Ask, "What conclusion or conclusions are suggested to you by your observations?"

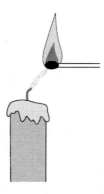

Figure 1: Relight a candle by holding a lighted match over the white smoke from a just-extinguished candle.

3. Form a tube of aluminum foil by rolling a 10-cm x 10-cm square of foil around a pencil. Remove the pencil and hold the foil tube with a test tube holder or spring clothespin, being very careful not to squash the tube. Carefully hold one end of the tube in the center of the flame at a 45–60° angle to the candle. Black smoke should be visible from the other end of the tube. (See Figure 2.) Touch a lighted match to this end of the tube and observe what happens. (The smoke should ignite.) Ask, "What conclusions are suggested by your observations?"

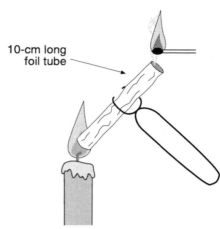

10-cm long
foil tube

Figure 2: Hold the end of an aluminum-foil tube to the center of a candle flame and hold a match in the smoke coming from the other end.

4. Hold the bottom of a wire kitchen strainer in the candle flame. Ask, "Does the flame burn below the wire? Does the flame burn above the wire? Can you suggest an explanation for your observation?"

5. Place a short, wide candle in a bowl and fill the bowl with water up to the rim of the candle. Light the candle. As it burns, the sides in contact with the water remain solid as the flame burns down inside the candle. Ask, "What does this suggest to you about how the candle burns?"

6. Place an inverted wide-mouthed glass bottle or jar over a burning candle. The flame goes out. Ask, "Why?" Time the event for two different-sized bottles. Ask, "Does the size of the vessel placed over the burning candle influence the time that elapses before the flame goes out? What conclusions are suggested to you by these results?"

7. Put a drop of water on a piece of blue cobalt chloride test paper. You should observe a color change from blue to pink. This color change indicates the presence of water. Now, carefully hold the opening of an inverted wide-mouthed glass bottle or jar above but near the flame of a burning candle. If this is done correctly, you will note the presence of a clear liquid on the inside of the bottle or jar. Test this liquid with blue cobalt chloride test paper. Ask, "What does this test suggest about the identity of this liquid? Can you explain your results?"

8. Cautiously hold a ceramic saucer just above a candle flame. Ask, "What observation do you make? Do your observations suggest the presence of any particular substance in the flame of a candle? If so, what substance is suggested?"

9. Place a large-diameter candle in a jar that contains a small amount of limewater (enough to fill the jar to a depth of about 2–3 cm). Light the candle with a long match and allow it to burn for at least 30 seconds. Place the lid on the jar and allow the flame to go out.

Gently shake the jar. A white precipitate should form. Perform a control by adding limewater to a second jar containing an unlit candle, then covering and shaking. Is a precipitate formed in this second case? Using a straw, blow air through the limewater in the second jar. Limewater is used to test for the presence of carbon dioxide gas. Ask, "What do your results suggest about the identity of at least one of the products produced when a candle burns?"

10. Using the apparatus shown in Figure 3, determine the amount of heat produced per gram of candle burned as follows:

   a. Determine the individual masses of a candle, an empty soup can, and the same soup can with 250 mL (1 cup) water in it. Also measure the initial temperature of the water. Calculate the mass of the water:

   $$mass_{(can+water)} - mass_{(can)} = mass_{(water)}$$

   b. Light the candle and use it to heat the water in the soup can.

   c. Heat the water for 5–10 minutes (Do not allow it to boil) and monitor the temperature of the water. Record the highest temperature reached during heating.

   d. Blow out the candle and determine the mass of the remaining candle.

   e. Calculate the temperature change (ΔT) of the water:

   $$T_{final} - T_{initial} = \Delta T$$

   f. Calculate the mass of the candle burned:

   $$mass_{initial} - mass_{final} = mass\ lost$$

   g. Calculate the calories gained by the water:

   $$calories = mass_{water} \times specific\ heat_{water} \times \Delta T$$

➤ **The specific heat of water is 1 calorie/g °C. Calories gained by the water equals calories produced by the candle.**

   h. Calculate the calories produced per gram of candle burned by dividing the calories produced by mass of candle lost.

   i. Repeat Steps 10a–10h using other types of candles. Allow the can to cool to about the same initial temperature as in the first trial before performing the experiment with a different candle.

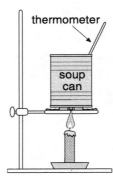

Figure 3: The apparatus for determining the heat produced per gram of candle burned

Explanation

For a detailed discussion of candle making and the chemistry of combustion, see the Content Review and Activity 2, "Making Candles." A specific explanation for each investigation follows.

1. **Finding what is consumed as a candle burns:** Wax, and not just the wick, is consumed as a fuel when candles burn. Supporting evidence includes the observations that the candle itself decreases in size as it burns and that candles of different diameter decrease in height at different rates according to the quantity of wax available for burning. The fact that a pool of liquid wax forms at the base of the wick indicates that wax is melted by the heat of the flame.

2. **Relighting a just-extinguished candle from a distance:** Wax burns as a vapor. The white smoke rising from a candle that has just been extinguished is actually a mixture of wax vapor and recondensed wax vapor (solid or liquid). The gaseous wax will relight if it is ignited before it either disperses or cools enough to condense.

3. **Lighting the smoke from a burning candle:** The gas pipe formed from aluminum foil shows that the substance that burns (wax vapor) is present in the flame and will travel through the pipe and burn. The visible smoke is a mixture of solid combustion products, including soot.

4. **Putting a strainer in a candle flame:** When a kitchen strainer is placed in the candle flame, the metal conducts the flame's heat away from the flame and the fuel (the paraffin vapor). This allows the paraffin vapor to cool below its kindling temperature. Thus, the wax vapor that has passed through the strainer does not remain ignited.

5. **Burning a candle that is surrounded by water:** The sides of the candle remain intact because heat is conducted away from the outside of the candle by the water. Hence, the outside layer of wax cannot melt, vaporize, and burn.

6. **Placing a vessel over a burning candle:** Students may offer a variety of explanations for why the flame goes out. Some may guess that the combustion process produces a gas that suffocates the flame. Although this answer is incorrect, it cannot be disproved by this experiment, so it is not an unreasonable guess.

   Flames require a certain minimum amount of oxygen to burn. If the amount of oxygen available to a flame falls below this minimum amount, the flame dies. When you place a vessel over the flame, the flame begins to consume the oxygen present in the vessel, and no new oxygen is available to replace the oxygen used up by the flame. Therefore, the oxygen concentration in the air falls and the flame goes out. A larger vessel contains more oxygen; thus, the flame takes longer to consume the oxygen.

7. **Holding a vessel above but near the candle flame:** The water vapor produced during combustion condenses on the cold glass. The liquid can be identified as water by testing with cobalt chloride test paper which turns from blue to pink in the presence of water. This result should be compared with the effect of a sample of water on the paper.

8. **Holding a ceramic saucer over a candle flame:** Holding a saucer in the middle of the candle flame results in carbon deposits (soot) forming on the saucer.

9. **Burning a candle in a jar with limewater:** This investigation enables you to collect hot carbon dioxide from the flame. When the jar is shaken, the gaseous carbon dioxide reacts with limewater in the following way:

$$Ca(OH)_2\ (aq)\ +\ CO_2\ (g) \longrightarrow CaCO_3\ (s)\ +\ H_2O\ (l)$$

limewater   carbon   calcium   water
dioxide   carbonate

Figure 4: Reaction between limewater and carbon dioxide

The formation of solid white calcium carbonate ($CaCO_3$) causes the limewater to turn white. No gas other than carbon dioxide will produce a solid in limewater. Carbon dioxide is also present in human breath, which is why the limewater turns white after you blow through it. The limewater in the control beaker does not turn white before breath is blown through the jar because air contains only a small amount of carbon dioxide, not enough to form appreciable amounts of the white solid.

10. **Determining the amount of heat produced per gram of candle burned:** The heat lost by the candle is absorbed by the water. Students use the formulas provided to calculate the amount of heat lost by the candle during the combustion process. While the assumption made in using this formula is that an insignificant amount of the heat is lost to the environment, it should be pointed out that in reality, significant heat is lost to the air in the experiment.

Key Science Concepts

* combustion
* heat production

Cross-Curricular Integration

Mathematics
Have the students do Investigation 10 and graph the calories produced per gram of candle for various types of candles used.

References

Hans Jurgen Press. *Simple Science Experiments;* Discovery Toys: USA, 1967.

"Investigating a Burning Candle;" *Fun with Chemistry: A Guidebook of K–12 Activities;* Sarquis, M., Sarquis, J., Eds.; Institute for Chemical Education: Madison, WI, 1992; Vol. 2, pp 339–346.

Wyatt, C., Colerain High School, personal communication.

Making Cleansing Cream

How is cleansing cream made? Why does it remove makeup so well? This activity allows students to prepare their own cleansing cream and answer these questions.

Recommended Grade Level .... **9–12 as a hands-on activity**
4–8 as a demonstration
Group Size .... **2–4 students**
Time for Preparation .... **15 minutes**
Time for Procedure .... **45 minutes**

Materials

Opening Strategy
- commercial cleansing cream

Procedure
Per Group
- 25.0 g paraffin wax
- 2.0 g laundry borax (sodium tetraborate decahydrate, $Na_2B_4O_7 \cdot 10H_2O$)
- 2.0 g Emersol NF 132 Lily Stearic Acid
- 155 mL (about ⅔ cup) mineral oil (not mineral spirits)
- balance
- 1 of the following sources of heat:
  - hot plate
  - Bunsen burner with ring stand, ring clamp, wire gauze, and an 800-mL to 1-L beaker
- stirring rod or stirring stick
- 400-mL beaker
- 250-mL beaker
- 100-mL graduated cylinder
- watch glass for 400-mL beaker, or wet cloth
- 2 thermometers
- container for cleansing cream (e.g., margarine tub, Styrofoam™ cup, etc.)
- (optional) cheese grater
- (optional) plastic bags
- (optional) 5–10 drops perfume
- goggles

Variation
Per Group
- 1 Tbsp fine sand or pumice
- electric or hand mixer for beating mixture

4

Extension

Per Class
- egg
- ½ tsp table salt
- ¼ tsp dry mustard
- ⅛ tsp paprika
- 1 Tbsp vinegar
- 1 cup salad oil
- small mixing bowl
- fork, whisk, or mixer
- measuring cup and spoons
- different brands of commercial regular and "lite" mayonnaise

Resources

Paraffin wax, stearic acid, and mineral oil can be purchased from a chemical supply company such as Flinn Scientific, P.O. Box 219, Batavia, IL 60510-0219, 800/452-1261.

- paraffin wax—catalog # P0003 for 500 g
- stearic acid—catalog # S0335 for 100 g
- mineral oil—catalog # M0065 for 4 L

The Emersol NF 132 Lily Stearic Acid can be obtained from Henkel Corporation, Emery Group, Attn: Jon Heimann, 4900 Este Avenue, Cincinnati, OH 45232, 513/482-2401.

Laundry borax, paraffin wax, and mineral oil can also be purchased at a grocery store.

Safety and Disposal

Goggles should be worn when performing this activity.

Paraffin wax is flammable. The wax should not be heated above 95°C (203°F) as it may ignite. Mineral oil is also flammable. Do not leave the paraffin wax or mineral oil unattended while heating. If either paraffin or mineral oil ignites, cover the beaker with a watch glass or wet cloth to shut off the air supply to the fire.

Some people have developed an allergic reaction to dry, powdered borax. Use care when handling it. Avoid inhalation and ingestion. Use adequate ventilation in preparing the borax solution and wash your hands after contact with the solid.

The materials used in this activity are intended for external use only. Persons with especially sensitive skin or known allergies to any of the cold cream ingredients should avoid contact with the cold cream. Do not use the cleansing cream on the face or other delicate areas of the body. It is appropriate to use the cleansing cream on the hands. Once the activity is completed, any unwanted cleansing cream can be discarded in the waste basket.

If doing the Extension (which involves tasting), be sure not to use ingredients, measuring utensils, or cooking equipment that have been used in a lab or stored among laboratory chemicals. Impress upon the students that this experiment is an exception to the rule that they should never taste materials used in a chemistry experiment—in most cases, they should not taste anything used or produced in a chemistry class or other science class.

Getting Ready

To decrease the time it takes for the paraffin wax to melt, break up the paraffin into small chunks or grate it using a cheese grater. Especially for younger students, it may be convenient to pre-weigh the paraffin and place it in labeled plastic bags.

Opening Strategy

Show students a jar of cleansing cream. Ask students how the product is used. Have them describe its properties (e.g., texture, appearance). Ask students to suggest possible ingredients based on their knowledge of the uses of the cleansing cream and the cleansing cream's appearance.

Procedure

Students should do this Procedure in pairs or larger groups. Half the group will do Step 1 while the other half does Step 2. Each group will then work together to complete Steps 3–7.

1. Prepare the paraffin wax as follows:

Paraffin is flammable. It should not be heated above 95°C (203°F) in the next step. See Safety and Disposal.

   a. Weigh 25.0 g paraffin wax and place it into a 400-mL beaker. Place the beaker and its contents on a hot plate and use medium to high heat to melt it.

   b. Weigh out 2.0 g stearic acid on a piece of paper and set it aside.

   c. When the paraffin has melted, remove the beaker from the heat source and add the stearic acid to the paraffin. Stir the mixture with a stirring rod or stirring stick.

Mineral oil is flammable. See Safety and Disposal.

   d. Pour 155 mL mineral oil into the paraffin/stearic acid mixture in the 400-mL beaker.

   e. Return the 400-mL beaker and its contents to the hot plate. While monitoring the temperature of the mixture with a second thermometer, heat the mixture to 70°C (158°F).

2. Prepare the borax solution as follows:

   a. Pour 90 mL water into a clean 250-mL beaker. Put the beaker of water on the hot plate.

   b. Weigh out 2.0 g laundry borax (sodium tetraborate decahydrate, $Na_2B_4O_7 \cdot 10 H_2O$) and pour it into the water in the 250-mL beaker. Stir the solution with a stirring rod or stirring stick until the solid dissolves completely.

   c. While monitoring the temperature with a thermometer, heat the borax solution to 65°C (149°F).

3. Once the borax solution from Step 2 has reached 65°C (149°F), pour this solution into the paraffin/stearic acid/mineral oil solution in the 400-mL beaker from Step 1, stirring continuously.

4. (optional) Add 5–10 drops of perfume.

5. Remove the beaker from the heat and continue stirring until the temperature drops to 40°C (104°F), preferably lower.

6. Pour the mixture (your homemade cleansing cream) into a margarine tub or large Styrofoam cup while it is still liquid.

 It is not a good idea to use the cleansing cream on the face or other delicate areas of the body. Most people can use the cleansing cream on the hands. Persons with especially sensitive skin or known allergies to any of the cold cream ingredients should avoid contact with it.

7. Make observations about the cold cream using the senses of touch, smell, and sight. Compare the homemade cold cream to commercial cold cream.

Variation

Repeat the activity, but add 1 Tbsp of fine sand or pumice to the cleansing cream; this makes a good "waterless hand cleaner."

Extension

Have the class make a tasty emulsion—mayonnaise is an emulsion of oil in vinegar with the lecithin in egg yolk serving as the emulsifying agent.

1. Put an egg yolk, ½ tsp salt, ¼ tsp dry mustard and ⅛ tsp paprika in a small bowl and beat thoroughly with a fork, whisk, or electric or hand mixer.

2. Add 1 Tbsp vinegar and beat again.

3. Very gradually, beat in 8 oz (1 cup) salad oil, adding only ½ tsp at a time for the first 2 oz. Then add ½ oz at a time until all of the oil is added.

Have the students compare the taste, texture, and color of their homemade mayonnaise to commercial brands of regular and "lite" mayonnaise to see if there are any differences.

Discussion

- Ask the students to compare the homemade cleansing cream to the commercial cleansing cream.
  The homemade product is greasier, which makes it harder to rinse off. The commercial product has a silkier texture.

- Discuss the role of the stearic acid in the cleansing cream.
  The cleansing cream is made from a suspension of small droplets of the paraffin and mineral oil in the water. The stearic acid acts as an emulsifying agent so that the paraffin and mineral oil can mix with the water to form a stable distribution of particles.

Explanation

While oil and water don't typically mix, adding stearic acid can cause the oil to become suspended in the water, forming an emulsion. An emulsion is the stable suspension (or colloid) of one liquid within another. Cleansing cream is an emulsion of paraffin wax and mineral oil in water. Stearic acid acts as a surfactant, or surface-active agent, as well as an emulsifying agent. An emulsifying agent facilitates the suspension of one liquid in another. Because the paraffin wax and mineral oil are not soluble in water, the emulsifying agent, stearic acid, stabilizes small drops of the paraffin wax and mineral oil which can then be suspended in the water. The droplets are small enough to be colloidal and therefore do not settle out. An emulsion is a liquid-in-liquid colloid. These droplets are too small to see, but they scatter light, which makes the cleansing cream opaque.

Cleansing creams work because they combine the cleaning abilities of oils and water. The oil drops dissolve greasy dirt and water dissolves water-soluble substances on the skin. All the dirt is removed when the cream is wiped off the skin.

Key Science Concepts

- emulsions
- solubility

Cross-Curricular Integration

Language Arts
Have the students read the short story *How Beautiful with Mud* from the collection *More Chucklebait: Funny Stories for Everyone,* by Margaret Scoggin (Knopf, 1949). Discuss the need for truth in advertising, product value (utility), etc.

References

Creek, B.F. "Higher Costs Spur New Detergent Formulations," *Chemical and Engineering News.* 1989, 67(4), 29–49.

"Food for Thought: Dispersion Recipes from the WonderScience Kitchen," *WonderScience.* 1987, 1(4), 8.

Scott, A. *Molecular Machinery;* Blackwell: Oxford, OH, 1989.

Summerlin, L.R.; Borgford, C.L.; Early, J.L. *Chemical Demonstrations, A Sourcebook for Teachers;* American Chemical Society: Washington, D.C., 1988; Vol. 2.

Preparation and Comparison of Four Soaps

How is soap made? Are all soaps made with the same materials? Do all soaps lather the same? This activity involves making different kinds of soaps from lard and from commercially available fatty acids and then comparing their properties.

Recommended Grade Level .... **9–12 as a hands-on activity**
4–8 as a demonstration
Group Size .... **1–4 students**
Time for Preparation .... **10–20 minutes**
Time for Procedure .... **Part 1: 45–60 minutes per recipe**
Part 2: 20–30 minutes

Materials

Procedure, Part 1

Per Group (for each soap recipe)
- 250-mL beaker
- 400-mL beaker
- 10-mL graduated cylinder
- 100-mL graduated cylinder
- stirring rod
- small spoon or spatula
- watch glass for 250-mL beaker
- balance
- hot plate (stirring model, if available)
- goggles

Per Class
- ice bath

Lard Soap
- 10 g lard
- 15 g solid sodium hydroxide (NaOH)
- 50 g table salt (sodium chloride, NaCl)
- 20 mL rubbing alcohol (70% isopropyl alcohol solution)
- 400 mL water

Stearic Acid Soap
For sodium soap
- 13.8 g Emersol 132 NF Lily Stearic Acid
- 8.5 mL 6 M sodium hydroxide solution (NaOH) purchased or made as described in Getting Ready
- 85 mL water

For potassium soap
- 13.1 g Emersol 132 NF Lily Stearic Acid
- 8.1 mL 6 M potassium hydroxide solution (KOH) made as described in Getting Ready
- 85 mL water

Oleic Acid Soap
For sodium soap
- 13.8 g Emersol 221 NF Oleic Acid
- 8.5 mL 6 M sodium hydroxide solution (NaOH)
- 85 mL water

For potassium soap
- 13.1 g Emersol 221 NF Oleic Acid
- 7.9 mL 6 M potassium hydroxide solution (KOH)
- 85 mL water

Coconut Fatty Acid Soap
For sodium soap
- 13.5 g Emery 622 Coconut Fatty Acid
- 11.0 mL 6 M sodium hydroxide solution (NaOH)
- 85 mL water
- small bottle
- hot-water bath

For potassium soap
- 12.7 g Emery 622 Coconut Fatty Acid
- 10.2 mL 6 M potassium hydroxide solution (KOH)
- 85 mL water
- small bottle
- hot-water bath

Procedure, Part 2
Per Group (for each sample tested)
- sample of the soap prepared or sample of commercial soap or detergent
- teaspoon measure
- 20 mL rubbing alcohol (70% isopropyl alcohol)
- 20 mL 0.1 M calcium chloride solution ($CaCl_2$) purchased or made as described in Getting Ready
- 5–10 drops 0.01 M sodium hydroxide solution (NaOH)
- 2 drops phenolphthalein indicator
- 100-mL graduated cylinder
- 50-mL beaker
- hot plate
- goggles

Resources

Sodium hydroxide, potassium hydroxide, ethyl alcohol, and calcium chloride can be purchased from a chemical supply company such as Flinn Scientific, P.O. Box 219, Batavia, IL 60510-0219, 800/452-1261.

- solid sodium hydroxide pellets—catalog # S0075 for 500 g
- 6 M sodium hydroxide solution—catalog # S0242 for 500 mL
- 0.1 M calcium chloride solution—catalog # C0234 for 500 mL
- solid potassium hydroxide pellets—catalog # P0059 for 500 g
- phenolphthalein indicator—catalog # P0019 for 100 mL
- calcium chloride—catalog # C0196 for 100 g

Various fatty acid mixtures required in this activity can be obtained from Henkel Corporation, Emery Group, Attn: Jon Heimann, 4900 Este Avenue, Cincinnati, OH 45232, 513/482-2401.

Lard and solid sodium hydroxide (lye) can be purchased from a grocery store.

Safety and Disposal

Goggles must be worn when performing this activity. Dust, pellets, and solutions of sodium hydroxide (NaOH) and potassium hydroxide (KOH) are very caustic. Both hydroxides can cause severe chemical burns and destroy cell membranes. Contact with the skin and the eyes must be prevented. Should contact occur, rinse the affected area with water for 15 minutes. If the contact involves the eyes, medical attention should be sought while the rinsing is occurring.

Do not prepare sodium hydroxide and potassium hydroxide solutions in containers made of "regular" glass such as a pitcher, drinking glass, or other thick non-Pyrex® container. The heat generated might cause the glass to crack, spilling the caustic solution, especially when the hot container is placed in an ice bath.

Preparation of sodium hydroxide and potassium hydroxide solutions is very exothermic. Have an ice bath available. When preparing these solutions, always add the solids to water. When all the solid is dissolved and the solution cools somewhat, it can be diluted to the desired final volume with water. The unused sodium hydroxide or potassium hydroxide solutions can be saved for future use or diluted with water and flushed down the drain.

Isopropyl alcohol is intended for external use only. It is flammable; keep flames away.

The soaps made in this activity are not meant for use in washing the sensitive parts of the body because excess lye may be present. After the activity has been completed, discard soap in the trash.

Getting Ready

Precise concentrations of the following solutions are not critical for this activity. Use the following procedures to prepare the necessary solutions.

 If a sodium hydroxide solution is prepared, the beaker and sodium hydroxide solution will become very hot! The flask or beaker must be placed in the ice bath.

- If a 6 M sodium hydroxide solution (NaOH) is not purchased, a solution can be prepared by dissolving 240 g solid sodium hydroxide in 1 L water. Use caution in preparing and handling. (See Safety and Disposal.)

 If a potassium hydroxide solution is prepared, the beaker and potassium hydroxide solution will become very hot! The flask or beaker must be placed in the ice bath.

- Prepare a 6 M potassium hydroxide solution (KOH) by dissolving 337 g solid potassium hydroxide pellets in 1 L water. Use caution in preparing and handling. (See Safety and Disposal.)

- Prepare a 0.1 M calcium chloride solution ($CaCl_2$) by dissolving 1.67 g calcium chloride in 150 mL water.

- Prepare a 0.01 M sodium hydroxide solution (NaOH) as follows: Prepare a 1 M sodium hydroxide solution by diluting 8.3 mL 6 M sodium hydroxide solution to a volume of 50 mL, then add 0.5 mL (10 drops) 1 M sodium hydroxide solution to 50 mL water.

Emery 622 Coconut Fatty Acid melts near room temperature. Before using the fatty acid to make soap, a sample must be melted to assure homogeneity. This can be accomplished by placing a sample of the coconut fatty acid in a small bottle and placing it in a hot-water bath or a sink containing hot water.

Opening Strategy

Discuss the early American history of soap-making with the students. (See Explanation for details.)

Procedure

 Do not use the thermometer to stir mixtures as it is fragile.

Part 1: Preparation of the Soaps

 So that the all the different soaps can be created within a given class period, you may wish to assign each group a different soap to make and have the groups compare the products. Some of the soaps will be solid, some will be liquid.

A: Lard Soap
1. Place 50 g table salt (sodium chloride, NaCl) and 175 mL water into a 400-mL beaker and stir to dissolve.

 Solid sodium hydroxide (NaOH) and concentrated solutions of it are very caustic. Use extreme caution in the next step. See Safety and Disposal.

2. Using a small spoon or spatula, place 15 g solid sodium hydroxide into a 250-mL beaker containing 10 g lard, 20 mL rubbing alcohol (70% isopropyl alcohol solution), and 20 mL water. Stir the mixture with a stirring rod.

Do not use an open flame when heating the mixture in the next step. Rubbing alcohol is flammable.

3. Use a hot plate to heat the 250-mL beaker and its contents, stirring until the mixture comes to a gentle boil. Continue heating until the lard is dissolved. If necessary, add water to the beaker to keep the volume approximately constant.

4. When the contents of the 250-mL beaker are entirely liquid, pour them into the 400-mL beaker containing the salt solution. As the contents of the beaker cool, soap will form on the surface of the liquid.

Do not handle the soap with your hands until it has been rinsed with water as it still contains excess base.

5. After 1 hour (or overnight depending on the time constraints), pour off the solution in the 400-mL beaker and rinse the remaining soap in approximately 200 mL tap water. The soap will be semi-solid.

B: Stearic Acid Soap

1. Place 13.8 g stearic acid into a 250-mL beaker and use a hot plate to warm it at a fairly low heat setting to melt the stearic acid.

The 6 M sodium hydroxide solution (NaOH) is very caustic. Use extreme caution in the next step. (See Safety and Disposal.)

2. Mix 8.5 mL 6 M sodium hydroxide solution and 85 mL water in a 400-mL beaker. Warm the diluted sodium hydroxide solution to about 50°C.

3. When the stearic acid has melted, pour it into the 400-mL beaker containing the warm sodium hydroxide solution and stir.

> **A curdy white precipitate forms which re-dissolves in Step 4 to give a smooth, viscous mixture. The mixture will not be clear due to suspended air bubbles.**

4. Heat the mixture for about 40 minutes total to complete the reaction. Keep the temperature below 85°C to minimize the possibility of the solution boiling over. Add water as needed to keep the total volume constant.

5. Remove the beaker from the heat. Allow the solution to cool for 1 hour.

> **As the solution begins to cool, the air bubbles rise to the top revealing a clear solution. When the solution cools sufficiently, the soap will cloud and then solidify. The soap can set out overnight (or longer) without harm. If you want to hasten the solidification process, pour a little of the solution into a watch glass. The soap in the beaker may have a "skin" on top which can be scraped off and washed down the drain.**

C: Oleic Acid Soap

1. Place 13.8 g oleic acid in a 250-mL beaker.

The 6 M sodium hydroxide solution (NaOH) is very caustic. Use extreme caution in the next step. (See Safety and Disposal.)

2. Mix 8.5 mL 6 M sodium hydroxide solution and 85 mL water in a 400-mL beaker. Warm the diluted sodium hydroxide solution to about 50°C.

3. Add the oleic acid to the warm sodium hydroxide solution in the 400-mL beaker and stir.

> **Observations of the oleic acid soap are similar to those for stearic acid soap except that more foaming occurs.**

4. Heat the soap solution for approximately 40 minutes. Keep the temperature of the soap solution below 85°C to minimize the possibility of the solution boiling over. Add water as needed to keep the total volume constant.

5. Remove the beaker from the heat. Allow the solution to cool.
On standing overnight, the soap sets to a gel, but does not solidify.

D: Coconut Fatty Acid Soap

1. Place 13.5 g Emery 622 Coconut Fatty Acid in a 250-mL beaker.

The 6 M sodium hydroxide solution (NaOH) is very caustic. Use extreme caution in the next step. (See Safety and Disposal.)

2. Mix 11 mL 6 M sodium hydroxide solution and 85 mL water in a 400-mL beaker.

3. Stir and heat this diluted sodium hydroxide solution to between 45–50°C.

4. Add the coconut fatty acid to the warm sodium hydroxide solution in the 400-mL beaker.
A precipitate will form which redissolves with stirring and heating in Step 5.

5. Heat the soap solution for 40 minutes, stirring periodically. Keep the temperature of the solution below 85°C to minimize the possibility of the solution boiling over. Add water as needed to keep the total volume constant.

6. Remove the soap from the heat and allow it to cool.
On standing, the soap remains liquid.

E: Potassium Soaps

1. To prepare potassium soaps for stearic acid, oleic acid, and coconut fatty acid, follow the same procedure from Parts B–D with potassium hydroxide (KOH) in place of sodium hydroxide (NaOH) in the following amounts:

Procedure Used	Type of Soap	Amount of 6 M Potassium Hydroxide Needed	Amount of Fatty Acid Needed
Part B	Potassium Stearic Acid Soap	8.1 mL	13.1 g
Part C	Potassium Oleic Acid Soap	7.9 mL	13.1 g
Part D	Potassium Coconut Fatty Acid Soap	10.2 mL	12.7 g

Part 2: Comparison of Soap Properties

To minimize the equipment needs, each group can test its own soap samples. Additional commercial soap samples can also be tested for comparison. About 1 tsp of each type of soap works well for comparison.

A: Lathering Ability

1. Place about 1 tsp of each type of soap made in Part 1 in a separate 100-mL graduated cylinder and label.

2. Add 30 mL water to each cylinder and shake each cylinder 25 times. Observe the relative amounts of lather formed by noting the volume marking to which the lather rises.

3. Rank the soaps in order from least lather to most lather.

4. Discard the solutions down the drain and rinse the graduated cylinders for use in Part B.

B: Behavior in Hard Water

"Hard" water contains calcium ions (Ca^{2+}) and magnesium ions (Mg^{2+}). The 0.1 M calcium chloride ($CaCl_2$) solution is artificial hard water and contains a much larger concentration of calcium ions than typical natural samples of hard water.

1. Place about 1 tsp of each type of soap made in Part 1 in a separate 100-mL graduated cylinder.

2. Add 20 mL 0.1 M calcium chloride solution to each cylinder.

3. Cover each cylinder with plastic wrap or a stopper to avoid spillage, and gently shake it 25 times. Look for the formation of solid precipitates. Record any observations.

C: Excess Alkali Test

Because of variations in the composition of the fatty acid samples, excess alkali can be present even after the soap-making is completed. In commercial batch soap-making, each batch is tested for excess alkali and the amount of each component is adjusted as needed.

Do not use an open flame when heating the alcohol in the next step. Rubbing alcohol is flammable.

1. Pour about 20 mL rubbing alcohol (70% isopropyl alcohol) into a small beaker and use a hot plate to heat it to a gentle boil.

2. Add 2 drops of phenolphthalein indicator to the hot rubbing alcohol solution and enough drops (very few) of 0.01 M sodium hydroxide solution (NaOH) to attain a VERY PALE pink color.

3. Stir in a small amount (about ⅛ tsp) of the soap to be tested and return the alcohol solution to a gentle boil.

4. Observe the color of the solution and record the observations.

5. Repeat Steps 1–4 for each soap sample made in Part 1.

Explanation

Preparation of Soaps

In the traditional way of making soap, animal fats were boiled in water with a base such as lye (sodium hydroxide, NaOH) which was purchased commercially or with potash (potassium carbonate, K_2CO_3) which was extracted from wood ashes with water. In the presence of hot water, the animal fats (which contain triglycerides) can be broken down to give fatty acids and glycerol (glycerin). However, because excess base is present, the reaction goes all the way to form soaps, which are salts of fatty acids. (See Figure 1.)

triglyceride + 3NaOH → glycerol + sodium salts of long-chain fatty acids (soap)

Figure 1: The traditional soap-making process

Because of the solubility of soap in water, a special technique is often used to remove it from solution. This technique is called "salting out." It involves the addition of sodium chloride (NaCl) to the solution mixture. "Salting out" is a special application of the common ion effect. This decreases the solubility of the soap in the solution and makes it easier to remove. Consequently, the soaps contain a small amount of sodium chloride remaining from this process. Additionally, the salt causes the glycerin to prefer associating with the salt-water-insoluble soap (which floats) rather than the salt water.

Part 1, A involved the traditional starting materials, lard and lye, and isolated the soap using the "salting out" technique. The isopropyl alcohol used in the activity would not have been part of the traditional soap-making recipe. By providing a medium in which lard and lye are both soluble, isopropyl alcohol promotes the reaction between lye and the triglycerides found in the lard so that it occurs in a reasonable time period. This method leaves the glycerol produced by the reaction in the soap.

Part 1, B–E involved the preparation of soap directly from fatty acids. The direct reaction of fatty acids with base saves the time required for the splitting of triglycerides found in fats like lard. Moreover, no glycerol is present in the soap, giving the soap better consistency.

The stearic acid soaps made in Part B are solids and are less soluble in water than other soaps. This is due to the structure of the stearic acid. Stearic acid is a saturated fatty acid, which means that the carbons in the stearic acid molecule are singly bonded to one another. (See Figure 2.) If mixing is sufficient, many air bubbles become trapped in the soap mixture. Ivory® bar soap floats because the air bubbles trapped within it decrease the density of the soap. Because of stearic acid soap's insolubility, bar soaps (solids) are used under conditions where the ratio of water to soap is high (e.g., in taking showers and baths).

The sodium (Na^+) oleic soap made in Part 1, C sets to a gel while the potassium (K^+) oleic soap is a liquid. The reason that the oleic acid soaps do not solidify is because oleic acid is an unsaturated fatty acid. Unsaturated fatty acids contain double bonds between carbons. (See Figure 2.)

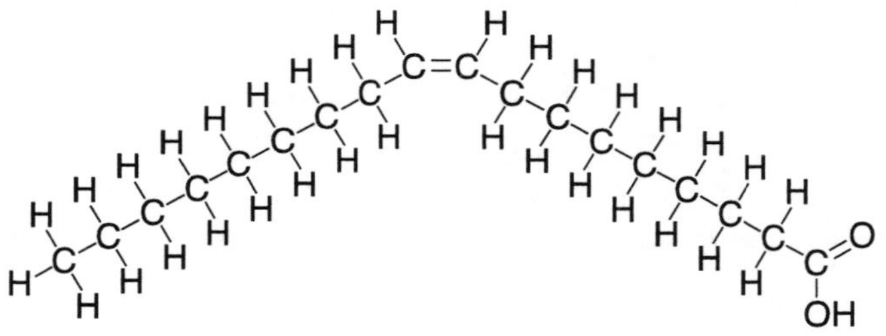

oleic acid
$CH_3(CH_2)_7CH=CH(CH_2)_7COOH$

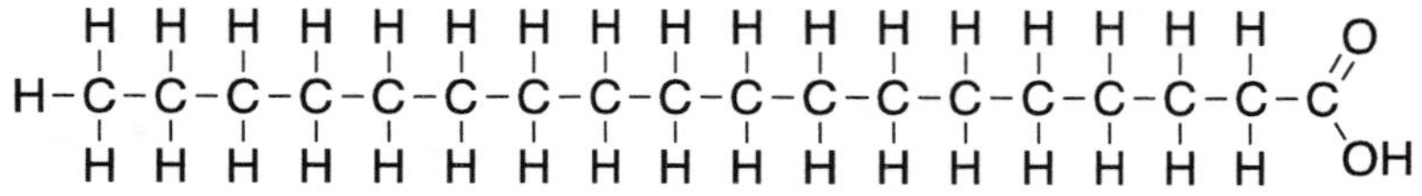

stearic acid
$C_{17}H_{35}COOH$

Figure 2: The structures of stearic and oleic acids

The geometry around the carbon-carbon double bond of oleic acid prevents efficient packing of the molecules and lowers the melting point compared to that of stearic acid. This is a general feature of unsaturated fatty acids. They are liquids at room temperature and so are the soaps produced from them.

The coconut fatty acid soaps made in Part 1, D are much more water soluble than the other soaps and therefore remain as a solution. This is due to the composition of the coconut fatty acid. It is a mixture of two short-chain fatty acids, lauric acid ($C_{11}H_{23}COOH$) and myristic acid ($C_{13}H_{27}COOH$). Although these two fatty acids are saturated like stearic acid, the smaller number of carbons and hydrogens gives the mixture a lower melting point. The soaps made from coconut fatty acids also have low melting points and are liquids at room temperature. Coconut fatty acid soaps are used in shampoos. Since the shorter chains in the coconut fatty acids make the soaps more soluble in water, they rinse away more easily.

Comparison of Soap and Detergent Properties

Lather consists of air bubbles trapped in soap solution. The stearic acid soaps and lard soap give very little lather. Progressively better lathering is seen with the oleic and coconut soaps. Oddly, the amount of lather has nothing to do with the ability of a soap to clean. Consumers just feel that a high volume of lather means that the soap "works" better.

In the hard-water test, the precipitates are calcium (Ca^{2+}) salts of fatty acids which are much less soluble than the sodium (Na^+) and potassium (K^+) salts. If commercial detergents are among the test items, no precipitate is observed. Detergents are synthetic chemicals, currently derived from petrochemicals and not from renewable natural resources (as soaps are). Fatty acids could be chemically modified or changed to become detergent starting materials but this is not presently done.

Detergents are salts of organic sulfonic acids. An example of a detergent is shown in Figure 3. The advantage of sulfonate salts is that they are more water-soluble than comparable fatty acid salts. Detergents also contain builders such as phosphates which complex with calcium (Ca^{2+}) and magnesium (Mg^{2+}) ions and keep them from forming precipitates. Common phosphate builders are sodium pyrophosphate ($Na_2P_2O_7$) and sodium trimetaphosphate ($Na_3P_3O_{10}$).

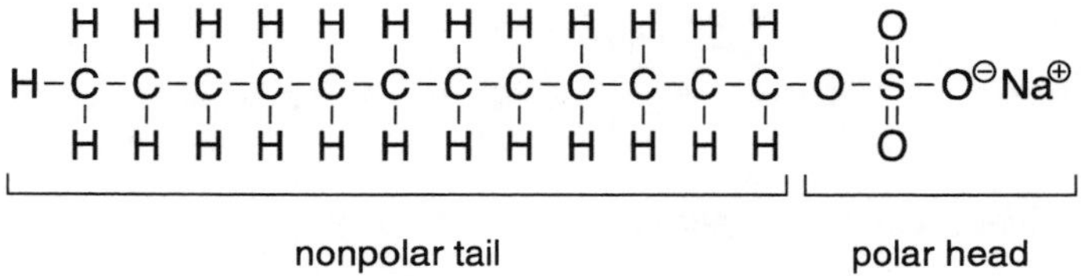

Figure 3: The structure of a detergent

The test for excess alkalinity is done in commercial soap-making. Because soaps are salts of weak acids, the pH of their solutions is not neutral (7), but rather on the basic side (9.0–9.5). The pale pink color of the alcohol solution before the soap is added is indicative of a pH around 9.0–9.5 with phenolphthalein. If the soap added contains unreacted strong base, the pH increases and the color becomes deeper red. If unreacted fatty acid is present, the pH decreases and the indicator becomes colorless. You should be aware, however, that the carbon dioxide in the air can also cause the phenolphthalein to decolorize. If beakers containing pale pink phenolphthalein are allowed to stand in the air, the color disappears due to absorption of carbon dioxide gas (CO_2) from the air which produces carbonic acid:

$$CO_2 + H_2O \rightleftharpoons H_2CO_3$$

carbon   water   carbonic
dioxide   acid

Figure 4: The reaction of carbon dioxide and water produces carbonic acid.

The History of Soap-Making

Home soap-making was common in America even until the earlier part of this century. Fat drippings were collected in a kettle on the back of the stove. Hot water was poured through wood ashes to get potash (potassium carbonate, K_2CO_3). When fat and potash were boiled together, the result was a harsh soap. Cut into bars for use in the home, this soap had a tendency to make hands rough and red because it was very difficult to add just the correct amount of potash to react with the fat so excess base was usually present. Those who could afford it bought lye (NaOH) to use instead of potash, but the inability to know exactly how much was needed and to weigh out these quantities remained a problem. Because of the effort required to make soap, it was a precious commodity on the American frontier.

The historic role of Cincinnati as a livestock market and butchering center for the surrounding agricultural area resulted in an abundant supply of beef fat (tallow) and pork fat (lard) and promoted the growth of industries such as the Emery Group of Henkel Corporation and Procter & Gamble. The first American soap maker was William Colgate, who established a laundry soap factory in New York City in 1806. Early American commercial soap makers such as Procter and Gamble (founded in Cincinnati in 1837) still made their soap outdoors in great iron kettles, but knew enough about chemistry to measure the correct proportions of fat and lye. They stirred the batches of boiling soap with a wooden paddle and poured the soap into wooden frames for hardening. The convenience of buying soap at a favorable price has supplanted its manufacture in the home.

References

American Chemical Society. *Chemistry in the Community;* Kendall/Hunt: Dubuque, IA, 1988; pp 58–63, pp 426–429.

Bramson, A. *Soap, Making It and Enjoying It,* 2nd ed.; Workman: New York.

Creek, B.F. "Higher Costs Spur New Detergent Formulations," *Chemical and Engineering News.* January 23, 1989, 29–49.

Kirk-Othmer Encyclopedia of Chemical Technology; Interscience: New York, 1966; Vol. 18, pp 415–443.

"Soaping Up," *Consumer Reports.* October 1990, 644.

Tocci, S. *Chemistry Around You;* Arco: New York, pp 107–109.

Surface Tension

Have you ever seen an insect walk across the surface of a pond? What kept it from sinking? Why does washing your hands with soap and water work better than washing with water alone? Surprisingly, these seemingly disparate questions are both related to a property of water known as surface tension. The investigations in this activity explore some characteristics of surface tension and demonstrate how soaps and detergents affect surface tension.

Recommended Grade Level **K–12**
Group Size .... **1–4 students or demonstration**
Time for Preparation .... **10–15 minutes**
Time for Procedure .... **30–50 minutes**

Materials

Opening Strategy
- sheet of acetate
- overhead projector
- dropper or disposable plastic pipet

Procedure, Part 1
Per Group or Demonstration
- tall, narrow glass or plastic cup
- a shallow pan (e.g., aluminum pie pan)
- dropper or disposable plastic pipet
- food color

Procedure, Part 2
Per Student
- penny
- dropper or disposable plastic pipet
- paper towel

Procedure, Part 3
Per Class
- quart jar with small mouth or milk bottle
- cheesecloth
- rubber band or string
- index card
- bucket or sink

Procedure, Part 4
Per Group or Demonstration
- large plastic cup
- dishwashing detergent

6

- dropper or disposable plastic pipet
- needle or paper clip
- fork
- cork

Procedure, Part 5

Per Group or Demonstration
- dishwashing detergent
- large plastic cup
- cotton string
- dropper or disposable plastic pipet
- scissors

Procedure, Part 6

Per Group or Demonstration
- 2 cotton balls
- 2 plastic cups
- dishwashing detergent
- dropper or disposable plastic pipet

Variation

For Part 1
- pennies or paper clips

For Part 3
- mason jar with screw lid
- screen
- (optional) toothpick
- scissors or wire cutters

For Part 5
- pepper

Resources

Medicine droppers and disposable plastic pipets can be purchased from a chemical supply company such as Flinn Scientific, P.O. Box 219, Batavia, IL 60510-0219, 800/452-1261.

- medicine dropper—catalog # GP7026 for package of 12
- disposable plastic pipets—catalog # AP1720 for package of 20

Opening Strategy

Put a sheet of acetate on the overhead projector. Drop several drops of water on the acetate. Ask students to describe each drop as it lands on the acetate. Ask them why water forms rounded beads instead of spreading out over the surface. Introduce the term "surface tension" by explaining that molecules of water are very attracted to each other (cohesion), and, in water, this force is greater than the force of attraction between the water and the acetate sheet (adhesion). Because of this strong cohesive force, water molecules form an elastic-like "skin" which pulls the water molecules into a bead. The measure of the strength of the cohesive force between the molecules on the surface of the water is called surface tension.

Procedure

Part 1: Overfilling a Glass

1. Place a glass or cup in a shallow pan and then carefully fill it just to the brim with colored water.

2. Using a dropper or disposable plastic pipet, add additional water. Count the number of drops that can be added before the cup overflows.

3. Allow students to poke the domed water surface with the point of a pencil to verify that the water seems to have a "skin."

Part 2: Drops of Water on a Penny

1. Place a penny head side up on a paper towel.

2. Predict how many drops of water can be placed on the penny before the water spills.

3. Count the number of drops that can be added to the penny's head-side surface without spilling. Describe the shape of the water as it sits on the surface of the penny.

4. Repeat Steps 1–3 using the tail side of the penny and compare the results.

Part 3: Surface Tension Demonstration

1. Cover the open mouth of an empty bottle or jar with two layers of cheesecloth, securing it with a rubber band or some string.

2. Pour water into the bottle through the cloth until the bottle is completely full.

3. Place an index card over the mouth of the bottle and quickly turn the bottle upside down over a bucket or sink.

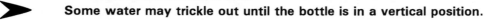 **Some water may trickle out until the bottle is in a vertical position.**

4. Carefully remove the index card and record your observations.

5. Tap the cheesecloth a few times with your finger and make observations.

Part 4: Sinking Objects with Detergent

1. Fill a cup with water.

2. Drop a cork on the surface of the water and observe that it floats.

3. Push the cork down and see that it rises again to the surface. Remove the cork from the cup.

4. Rest a needle or a paper clip on the tines of a fork.

5. Very carefully lower the tines of the fork into the water so that the needle or paper clip remains floating on the water. Slowly remove the fork without disturbing the needle or paper clip.

6. Push on the needle or paper clip to submerge it below the surface. Observe that the needle does not return to the surface.

7. Remove the needle or paper clip.

8. Float the needle or paper clip on the surface again as you did in Step 5.

9. Using a dropper or disposable plastic pipet, gently place a small drop of detergent onto the surface of the water. Continue to place drops of detergent in the water in a circle around the needle or paper clip until it sinks. (It may sink after the very first drop.)

Part 5: String Loop

1. Tie the ends of a short piece of string together to form a loop smaller than the diameter of the cup. Trim the loose ends of the string close to the knot.

2. Float the string loop on the surface of the water in the cup and note the shape that the loop forms.

3. Place a drop of detergent in the center of the loop and observe as the loop immediately becomes circular.

Part 6: Increasing Wettability With a Surfactant

1. Place approximately equal volumes of water in two cups.

2. Put a drop of detergent into the water of one of the cups.

3. Take two cotton balls and drop one into each cup. Observe the cotton balls.
The cotton ball in the cup containing detergent is wet by the water more quickly and sinks before the cotton ball in the cup containing only water.

Variations

For Part 1: Set a glass or cup in the pie pan and then carefully fill it just to the brim with colored water. Predict how many small objects, such as pennies or paper clips, can be added to the cup without spilling the water. Add pennies or paper clips to the cup of water and count the number of pennies or paper clips that are added before spilling the water. Compare the actual number to your prediction.

For Part 3: Prepare a jar for each group by cutting screen to fit inside the screw-on portion of the lid of a mason jar. Place the screen over the mouth of the jar and screw on the lid. Fill the jar completely full of water. Place an index card over the top of the screen and invert the jar over a sink or bucket. Remove the card and observe the surface of the screen. If desired, insert a toothpick through a hole in the screen. With the jar over a sink or bucket, tap the screen with your finger and observe what happens.

For Part 5: Fill a cup ¾-full with water. Sprinkle pepper onto the surface of the water until there is a uniform covering on the surface. Place one drop of detergent in the center of the water. Observe the motion of the pepper.

Discussion

For Parts 1–3:

- Ask students if the number of drops needed to overflow the cup or the penny was more than their prediction and why it took so many drops to get the water to overflow. *Because of the high surface tension of water, the cup and the penny can accommodate many drops before gravity overcomes the cohesive force between the molecules of water.*

- Ask students why the water stayed in the bottle even when it was inverted.
  The fibers of the cheesecloth provide the water with a large amount of surface area to which the water molecules can adhere. This force of the water molecules adhering to the fibers and the strong cohesive force between the water molecules is enough force to prevent gravity from pulling the water from the bottle. When you tap the cheesecloth, you disrupt the adhesive and cohesive forces, and gravity makes the water fall from the bottle.

For Parts 4–6:

- Ask students why the addition of detergent made the needle or paper clip sink.
  The high surface tension of water allows the needle or paper clip to rest on the surface of the water. When soap or detergent is added, the surface tension is "broken." The soap or detergent disrupts the cohesive forces between the water molecules, and the surface can no longer support the weight of the object.

- Ask students why the string loop became circular when the detergent was added to the center of the loop.
  When the detergent is added to the water, it forms a monolayer which disrupts the surface tension of the water at the point of entry of the detergent. As the monolayer disperses in all directions, the detergent disrupts more and more water molecules, causing the string loop to be pulled in all directions (making it circular) as the surface tension is weakened.

- Soaps and detergents decrease the surface tension of water. Ask students why this is important in cleaning.
  Because of water's high surface tension, it does not wet surfaces readily, and therefore it is difficult to clean things with plain water. In addition to solubilizing grease and dirt, soaps and detergents reduce the surface tension, allowing the water to wet surfaces more easily. This makes it easier to clean objects with soapy water than with plain water.

Explanation

Each of the six parts of this activity illustrates the surface tension properties of water. The super-full glass of water, the dome of water on the penny, and the floating needle are all possible because of the high surface tension of water.

Surface tension exists because of the attractive forces between molecules. Water molecules are attracted to each other; this attractive force between molecules is called cohesion. At the surface of a liquid, these cohesive forces cause molecules to be attracted to surrounding surface molecules, and to other molecules in the bulk of the liquid. (See Figure 1.) The strong cohesive forces in water make it act as if it has a "skin" on the surface.

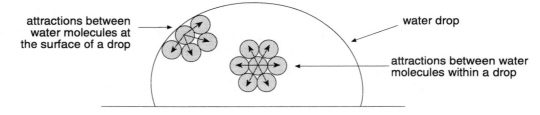

Figure 1: Representation of cohesive forces on molecules at two locations in a drop of water

Water has an especially high surface tension. This is because water molecules are polar, meaning that one end of the molecule has a net positive charge ($\delta+$), while the other end has a net negative charge ($\delta-$). (See Figure 2.) The polarity of water molecules enables the negative end of one molecule to be attracted to the positive end of its neighbor, producing a strong cohesive force.

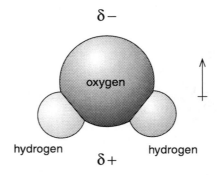

Figure 2: A model of a water molecule

Water's high surface tension causes it to "bead" when placed on a dry surface. Water forms a bead because the cohesive force tends to make the drop of water assume a spherical shape in order to minimize surface area for the volume. This phenomenon is illustrated in Parts 1 and 2. The dome formed by the water is due to the cohesive forces pulling the molecules into a spherical shape.

In Part 3, the water does not fall out of the bottle when it is inverted because the fibers of the cheesecloth provide the water with a large amount of surface area to which the water molecules can adhere. The force of attraction between water molecules and the fibers (called adhesion) and the strong cohesive force between the water molecules themselves is enough to prevent gravity from pulling the water from the bottle. When the cheesecloth is tapped, the adhesive and cohesive forces are disrupted, and gravity makes the water fall from the bottle.

Because water beads on dry surfaces, it is often difficult to clean with pure water because water won't wet surfaces very well. Surfactants (chemicals that decrease surface tension) must be added so that the water can adhere to or wet the surface to be cleaned. Soaps and detergents act as surfactants, which is one of the reasons that they make good cleansers. Soaps and detergents have one end that is hydrophilic (water-loving), or water-soluble, and one end that is hydrophobic (water-fearing), or insoluble in water. When detergent is added to a cup of water, it forms a monolayer (a film one molecule thick) on the surface with the hydrophilic ends immersed in the water and the hydrophobic ends sticking out. (See Figure 3.) This monolayer displaces the skin of water molecules, and there is no longer enough surface tension to support the weight of objects as seen in Parts 4 and 5. In Part 4, the needle or paper clip floated on the surface of the water, but sank as soon as the detergent was added.

In Part 5, as the monolayer of detergent placed in the center of the string loop disperses in all directions, the detergent disrupts more and more water molecules, causing the string loop to be pulled in all directions (making it circular) as the surface tension is depleted. The surface tension is broken only inside the loop where the detergent is. Outside the loop, strong cohesive forces exist in all directions.

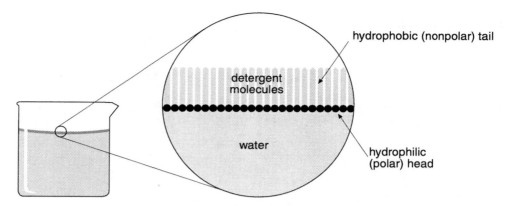

Figure 3: A detergent monolayer

Part 6 of this activity demonstrates that water containing detergent (and therefore having a lower surface tension) wets or adheres to the cotton ball better than plain water. This occurs because the surface tension has been disrupted, and the water can penetrate the minute spaces between the cotton fibers and soak it more quickly than plain water, which tends to form beads. When surface tension is low (in the presence of detergent), the energy of the adhesive forces can exceed the cohesive energy between water molecules and cause the surface of the cotton to become wet.

Key Science Concepts

- cohesion/adhesion
- intermolecular forces
- properties of water
- soaps/detergents/surfactants
- surface tension

Cross-Curricular Integration

Language Arts
Have students write stories describing one of the surface tension investigations from the point of view of a drop of water. Follow up by reading *The Magic School Bus at the Waterworks*, by Joanna Cole (Scholastic, ISBN 0-590-40360-5) to the class.

Mathematics
Have the students graph their results from Parts 1 and 2.

References

Almegren, F.J. Jr.; Taylor, J.E. "Geometry of Soap Films and Soap Bubbles," *Scientific American*. 1976, 235(18), 82–93.

American Chemical Society, *ChemCom: Chemistry in the Community;* Kendall-Hunt: Dubuque, IA, 1988; p 21.

Miller, F., Jr. *College Physics,* 4th ed.; Harcourt, Brace, Jovanovich: New York, NY, 1977; pp 596–599.

Blowing Bubbles

Students observe the shapes and colors of bubbles blown from a homemade bubble solution and compare them to bubbles blown from commercially prepared bubble solutions.

Recommended Grade Level K–12
Group Size .... 1–4 students or demonstration
Time for Preparation .... 10–15 minutes
Time for Procedure .... 30–50 minutes

Materials

Opening Strategy
- sheet of acetate
- overhead projector

Procedure
Per Class
- 315 mL (about 1⅓ cups) Joy®
- 1.75 L (about 7½ cups) water
- 100 mL (about ⅜ cup) glycerol (glycerin) solution
- 2-L bottle

Per Group
- about 100 mL bubble solution prepared as described in Getting Ready
- wire coat hanger
- 12-in length of heavy cotton string or rickrack
- shallow dish (e.g., aluminum pie pan)
- about 100 mL commercial bubble solution

Variations
- plastic pond
- hula hoop
- cement block
- coffee stirrers
- cotton string or pipe cleaners
- Kubic Bubbles kit

Resources

Glycerol can be purchased from a grocery or pharmacy as glycerin or from a chemical supply company such as Flinn Scientific, P.O. Box 219, Batavia, IL 60510-0219, 800/452-1261.

- glycerol solution—catalog # G0043 for 500 mL

The Kubic Bubbles kit can be purchased from a supply company like Frey Scientific, 905 Hickory Lane, Mansfield, OH 44905, 800/225-3739.

- Kubic Bubbles—catalog # 12128

Rickrack can be purchased at fabric stores. The other materials can be purchased at grocery, pharmacy, or hardware stores.

Safety and Disposal

Be sure students have enough room to swing wire bubble loops without the risk of hitting other students.

Getting Ready

Prepare the bubble solution by stirring 315 mL (1⅓ cups) of Joy®, 1.75 L (7½ cups) water, and 100 mL (⅜ cup) glycerol solution in a 2-L bottle. Store the bubble solution in the 2-L bottle and allow it to age for a week or more.

Bend each wire coat hanger into a loop so that the loop will fit in a shallow dish of bubble solution. (See Figure 1.) Wrap about a 12-in piece of cotton string or rickrack around the wire loop. (The string or rickrack is used to keep the loop wet with bubble solution.)

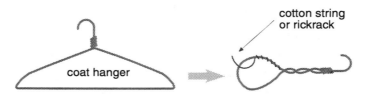

Figure 1: A coat hanger bubble loop

Opening Strategy

Put a sheet of acetate on the overhead projector. Drop several drops of water on the acetate. Ask the students to describe each droplet as it lands on the acetate. Ask them why water forms rounded beads instead of spreading out over the surface. Introduce the term "surface tension" by explaining that molecules of water are very attracted to each other (cohesion), and, in water, this force is greater than the force of attraction between the water and the acetate sheet (adhesion). Because of this strong cohesive force, water molecules form an elastic-like "skin" which pulls the water molecules into a bead. The measure of the strength of the cohesive force between the molecules on the surface of the water is called surface tension. Surface tension is also responsible for forming soap bubbles. Blow some bubbles using bubble solution and explain that the bubbles are round because the surface tension of the water causes them to form a sphere. A sphere has the smallest surface area for its volume of any shape.

Procedure

1. Half-fill (approximately 100 mL) a shallow dish with bubble solution (prepared in Getting Ready).

2. Dip the wire loop into the bubble solution and then carefully withdraw it so that the soap film supported on the rim of the loop is intact. (See Figure 2.)

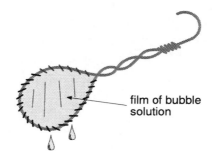

film of bubble solution

Figure 2: Bubble solution on the wire loop

3. Swing the loop so that a current of air extends the soap film into a bubble which soon pinches off and floats freely.

4. Observe the pulsating of the floating bubble's surface which eventually forms a spherical shape. Note the colors on the bubble's surface.

5. Try to make long, cylindrical bubbles by pulling the loop through the air. Note whether the bubbles stay cylindrical.

6. Repeat Steps 1–5 with commercial bubble solutions and compare the results.

Variations

- Encase a student in a bubble by having the student stand on a cement block in a plastic pond containing the bubble solution. Use a hula hoop as the bubble loop to generate the bubble.

- Make various three-dimensional shapes from coffee stirrers and cotton string or pipe cleaners, or use the Kubic Bubbles kit. Immerse the shapes in bubble solution and experiment with soap films of varying shapes.

Discussion

- Ask students to explain why bubbles are spherical.
  The soap/water membrane that makes up the bubble surface takes on the shape which minimizes its surface area for the volume.

- Ask students why a bubble bends when you blow on it.
  The surface of a bubble is two layers of soap with some water molecules trapped between the layers. When the bubble is subjected to a current of air, the surface area of the bubble increases, reducing the concentration of soap on that surface. With the larger surface area, water molecules migrate from the interior of the bubble to the outer layer, increasing the surface tension and pulling the stretched surface back together.

Explanation

The simple act of blowing a bubble is a consequence of some interesting science concepts. Any bubble formed is subject to two forces: 1) the surface tension tending to form the water into a sphere (since this is the shape in which there is minimum surface area for a given volume), and 2) the force of gravity which tends to make the water drain to the bottom of the bubble.

Soap is a surfactant—it lowers the surface tension of the water to which it is added. The surface tension is reduced by the surfactant because it occupies most of the surface, forcing water molecules (which have stronger attractive forces) into the body of the liquid. This same phenomenon occurs at the inner surface of the soap bubbles. (See Figure 3.)

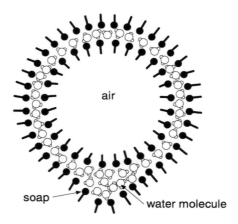

Figure 3: A cross-section of a soap bubble

Thus, when a surfactant is present, the minimum thickness of a bubble, shown in Figure 3, is limited to the thickness that can support two layers of surfactant, one on either surface. This counters the gravitational force, which would tend to make water flow from the top to the bottom part of the bubble, thinning the bubble wall at the top to the point of bursting. Nevertheless, given sufficient time, enough water drains to the bottom of the bubble to thin the top surface to the point of bursting. The purpose of adding glycerol to the soap bubble mixture is to increase the viscosity sufficiently to retard the draining of water and increase the bubble lifetime.

Now consider what happens when the bubble is subjected to a force such as a current of air which increases the surface, reducing the surfactant concentration. The increase in surface area allows some water molecules to migrate up from the interior of the bubble film, thus increasing the surface tension and pulling the surface back together. Conversely, contracting a portion of the surface increases the surfactant concentration, reduces the surface tension, and allows the surface to expand. This elastic behavior of the surface enables the bubble surface to respond to distortions so as to resist stretching and compression.

The same phenomenon accounts for the flattening effect of "pouring oil on troubled waters." The wind blows the water to make waves with tops that have an extended surface area. As previously described, the extended surface area allows some of the water molecules from below the surface to migrate to the surface. This causes the surface tension to increase and causes the wave to contract. This process continues as the wave motion builds. Pouring oil onto the water forms a thin film, lowers its surface tension, and forces water molecules below the surface, reducing the wave production.

What causes the colors exhibited by bubbles? A complete answer to this question involves a complicated combination of physical phenomena. Simply stated, the colors depend on the fact that a light beam of any particular wavelength is partly reflected from the surface and partly transmitted into the interior of the bubble. Light inside the bubble medium travels at a lower velocity than in air (refraction). When it reaches the inside wall of the bubble, part of the light wave is again reflected back toward the outside wall and part is reflected into the air inside the bubble. The reflection induces a phase shift in the light wave. Thus, depending on the wavelength of the light and the thickness of the bubble, the light beam may or may not be in phase with the original reflected beam when it reaches the outer surface of the bubble and is refracted from the bubble into the outside air. If the beams are perfectly out of phase, darkness results; if they are perfectly in phase, reinforcement of the two beams occurs and the color is intensified.

Since visible white light consists of a mixture of many wavelengths, the above considerations are true for each individual wavelength, and the observed colors will be determined by the mixture of reinforced colors at the outside bubble surface. In addition, the thickness of the bubble continually changes as the fluid drains from the top to the bottom under the force of gravity, thus changing the colors which reinforce and interfere. The development of different colors can be watched throughout the lifetime of the bubble. A pattern may repeat itself since a bubble thickness of any whole number of wavelengths produces interference while a thickness of a whole-number-plus-one-half wavelengths produces reinforcement. Intermediate situations occur between these two extremes for each wavelength.

Finally, let's consider why one can blow bubbles with the soap/glycerin/water solution (which has a lower surface tension than pure water) but not with pure water. This seems counter-intuitive since one might expect that the greater attraction of water molecules for one another would allow a pure-water bubble to have walls of greater strength.

Drops of pure water cannot exceed a certain (very small) size. When this small size is exceeded, the gravitational force due to the mass of the water overcomes the surface tension which holds the water in a spherical shape.

Of course, drops of water are different from bubbles since bubbles consist of a film surrounding air while drops are entirely water. We are still left with the question of why a film of pure water cannot surround a volume of air to form a stable bubble. The answer lies in the elasticity of the soap film—that is, its ability to expand and contract rather than disintegrate when subjected to deformations provided by air currents.

Key Science Concepts

- bubbles
- cohesion and adhesion
- soap/surfactant chemistry
- surface tension

Cross-Curricular Integration

Mathematics
Discuss the relationship between the volume and the surface area for different three-dimensional shapes. This will explain why bubbles are spherical.

References

Boys, C.V. *Soap Bubbles, Their Colours, and the Forces that Mold Them;* Dover: New York, 1959.

Cassidy, J. *The Unbelievable Bubble Book;* Klutz: Palo Alto, CA, 1987.

Faverty, J.; Faverty, R. *Professor Bubble's Official Bubble Handbook;* Greenleaf: Schenevus, NY, 1987.

Miller, F., Jr. *College Physics*, 4th ed.; Harcourt, Brace, Jovanovich: New York, 1977; pp 596–599.

Food Colors in Milk

What happens when you place food color and detergent in milk? The interaction of the detergent with the fat in milk results in a beautiful swirl of color that is bound to impress your students.

Recommended Grade Level **1–12**
Group Size .... **1–4 students**
Time for Preparation .... **5 minutes**
Time for Procedure .... **10 minutes**

Materials

Opening Strategy
- 2–3 drops food color
- transparent cup

Procedure
Per Group
- 1 of the following shallow, preferably transparent dishes:
  - saucer or shallow bowl
  - pill vial
  - small plastic cups
  - transparent film canister
  - top and bottom of a plastic petri dish, any size
- about 50 mL (about ½ cup) of whole milk and at least 1 of the following dairy products:
  - cream
  - half-and-half
  - 2% milk
  - 1% milk
  - buttermilk
  - skim milk
- liquid dishwashing detergent (enough to half-fill a 2-L bottle cap)
- food color (at least two different colors)
- at least 2 cotton-tipped swabs or a dropper

Extension
Per Class
- access to a stove or microwave oven
- access to a refrigerator

Resources

Petri dishes (culture dishes) can be purchased from a chemical supply company such as Flinn Scientific, P.O. Box 219, Batavia, IL 60510-0219, 800/452-1261.

- culture dishes—catalog # AP8170 for 20

Opening Strategy

Drop 2–3 drops of food color into a transparent cup of water. Ask the students to describe what is happening to the food color. (The food color sinks and begins to dissolve as it spreads throughout the water.) Then ask what would happen if you did the same thing to a glass of milk.

Procedure

1. Half-fill a shallow, transparent container with whole milk.

2. Place 1–2 drops of food color on the surface of the milk sample. Do not stir. Add 1–2 drops of a different food color to another part of the milk's surface. Add a third color of food color if desired. Without moving or shaking the container, observe both the top and sides. Record any observations about the drops of food color (For example, they spread out; they sink).

3. Touch one end of a dry cotton swab to a food color drop and observe what happens.

4. Wet the other end of the cotton swab in liquid dishwashing detergent and drip or gently touch the surface of the milk with this detergent. Record your observations. How long does the swirling continue?

 If the swirling motion stops, it can be started again by adding another drop of detergent to the center of the milk surface.

5. Repeat Steps 1–4 for a different type of milk sample to determine the effect that the fat content of the milk has on the swirling motion of the drops of food color.

Extension

- Investigate the effect of temperature on the swirling motion of the food color using warm milk, room-temperature milk, and cold milk.

Discussion

- Discuss possible reasons that the drops of food color did not spread out in the whole milk as they did in the water in the Opening Strategy.
  The fat in the whole milk immobilizes the drops and prevents them from diffusing throughout the milk.

- Discuss how the amount of milk fat affected the mobility of the food color drops before and after the liquid detergent was added.
  The more milk fat present in the milk, the more immobilized the food color drops would be and the less the food color drops would spread out during the swirling caused by the addition of the detergent.

Explanation

When water-soluble food color is added to water, it sinks to the bottom of the container and begins to spread and dissolve in the water because the food color is water-soluble. The observation is markedly different when the food color is placed on the surface of whole milk. The food color drops remain essentially intact on the surface of the whole milk with little or no spreading. While milk is largely water, it does contain, among other things, milk fat which exists as globules that are spread evenly throughout the milk. (This is caused by the homogenization process.) Because water-soluble food colors are not soluble in fats or oils, the fat globules retard the initial motion of the food color in the milk. The higher the fat content, the greater the initial immobility.

These contrasting observations result from the fact that water and fat are chemically very different. Water, a polar compound, dissolves compounds that are chemically like it. (Like dissolves like.) Water-soluble food colors are polar. Fats and oils, however, are nonpolar. While they dissolve in nonpolar solvents, they do not dissolve in water or other polar compounds. This difference in polarity results in little mixing between the water-soluble food color and the milk fat in the whole milk.

When soaps or detergents are added to the surface of the milk, the soap spreads out over the surface and causes the food color to swirl about. Several factors need to be considered to understand the cause of the swirling motion, including the nature of soap and fat molecules. Figure 1 shows the structure of sodium stearate, a common soap. Soap (and detergent) ions have two distinctly different parts. The long chain of carbon and hydrogen atoms is referred to as the nonpolar tail and the charged group on one end is called the polar head.

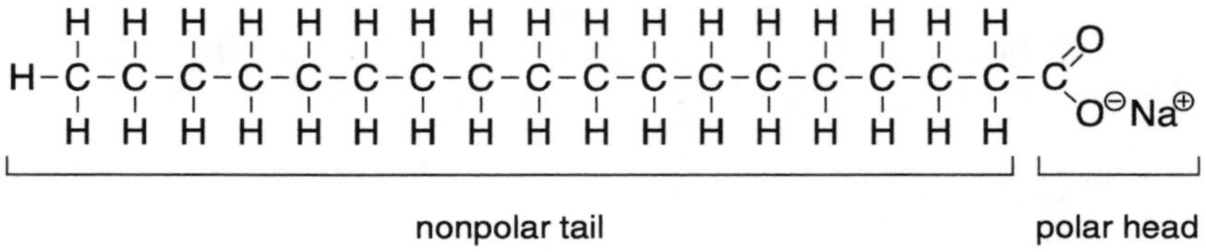

Figure 1: The structure of sodium stearate

Like the nonpolar tail of soap, fats and oils also contain large numbers of carbons and hydrogens in their structures. This similarity in structure allows the nonpolar tail of soap to dissolve in the globules of fats and oils, creating structures called micelles. Micelles look much like oranges with cloves poked through the rinds. (See Figure 2.) Part of the swirling and churning motion you see when you add soap to your dish of milk is a result of the attraction between the soap and the fat molecules in the milk.

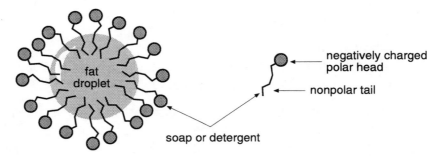

Figure 2: The absorption of fat into a soap micelle

As the soap spreads across the surface of the milk, more and more fat globules are pulled to the spreading soap. As these fat globules congregate, the water in the milk is pushed away, taking the food color with it. The movement in the milk will subside as the soap becomes "used up" (forming micelles). The addition of more soap can often reactivate the swirling and churning motion. Eventually, however, the system will reach equilibrium (the uniform distribution of the fat globule-soap micelles) and the motion will stop.

The following is a more detailed description of the chemistry of this system. First, the soap at low concentration forms a monolayer on the surface of the milk. This monolayer breaks the surface tension. The part of the milk's surface not yet covered by the monolayer of soap still draws the surface molecules into a minimum area, pulling the drops of food color across the surface. As the soap concentration increases enough to form a micelle, churning begins. A micelle is formed by the nonpolar tails of the soap clustering together. Figure 2 shows the nonpolar tails "hidden" inside the micelle and the charged, polar heads exposed to the water. The concentration of soap required for micelles to form is called the critical micelle concentration (cmc) and is usually quite small, typically around 0.01 molar.

As the soap dissolves in the water part of the milk, micelles of soap are formed. When the soap micelle encounters fats, oils, or grease, it dissolves the nonpolar material inside the micelle because of the "like dissolves like" attraction of the two. The fat globules encountered by the soap micelles are dissolved into the micelle. The soap micelle "pulls" the fat globules toward it because there is an attraction between the interior of the micelle and the fat. If large amounts of the fat globules are surrounded in this way, droplets of fat may remain suspended in solution. A suspension of a liquid in another liquid in which it is insoluble is called an emulsion. The soap serves as an emulsifying agent, promoting the suspension of the fat in the milk. If the amounts of insoluble material, in this case fat globules, are small enough, soaps act to increase the solubility of the fat globules in the milk.

Key Science Concepts

- emulsion
- micelles
- milk fat
- soaps/detergents

Cross-Curricular Integration

Art
Have students investigate the mixing of primary colors to make secondary colors through the swirling motion in the activity.

Language Arts
Have students write stories in which they are one of the drops of food color and describe how they are affected by the addition of the detergent drop.

Interview a grandparent, great-grandparent, or someone older in your family about how milk was obtained and packaged when they were young. Did they buy it in the store? Was it delivered? Did they milk cows? Was milk packaged the way it is today?

Life Science
Have students investigate the fat content in various types of milk products and discuss the nutritional value of dairy products and the health dangers of a high-fat, high-cholesterol diet.

Have students visit a grocery store and check the fat content on various food labels and plan a low-fat menu using some of the items they looked at.

Reference

"Mixable Unmixables," *WonderScience.* 1987, 1(4), 2–3.

Emulsifying Peanut or Vegetable Oil

Can you make oil and water mix? In this activity, oil and water mix when detergent is added.

Recommended Grade Level 4–12
Group Size .... 1–4 students
Time for Preparation .... 10 minutes
Time for Procedure .... 20–30 minutes

Materials

Opening Strategy
- 2 glass jars with lids
- about 480 mL (2 cups) vegetable oil
- about 240 mL (1 cup) mineral oil
- about 240 mL (1 cup) water

Procedure
Per Group
- 5 medium (15-mm x 125-mm) test tubes
- 5 corks or stoppers to fit test tubes
- test tube rack
- 10 mL (2 tsp) liquid dishwashing detergent
- 25 mL (1⅔ Tbsp) vegetable or peanut oil
- 25 mL (1⅔ Tbsp) water
- 10-mL graduated cylinder or a set of measuring spoons
- disposable, plastic pipet or dropper
- food color
- labels
- timing device with a second hand

Variation
- several brands of dishwashing detergent
- liquid hand soap

Safety and Disposal

Flush the oil/water mixtures down the drain with large amounts of water.

Opening Strategy

Fill two jars about half-full with vegetable oil. Ask the students to predict what will happen when mineral oil is added. Add mineral oil to one of the jars containing vegetable oil until the jar is about full. Cap the jar and invert it a few times. Observe. Ask the students to predict what will happen when water is added to the other jar of vegetable oil. Add the water, cap and invert as before. Observe. Compare the observations between the two jars.

Procedure

1. Label five medium test tubes with numbers 1–5. Add 5 mL water and a few drops of food color to each. Stopper and shake gently to mix.

2. Add 5 mL oil to each test tube. Observe the test tubes and record your observations.

3. Add drops of liquid dishwashing detergent to each of the test tubes according to the following table.

Table 1: Drops of Dishwashing Liquid To Be Added

Test Tube	Number of Drops
1	0
2	2
3	6
4	20
5	50

4. Stopper Test Tube 1 and shake it 10 times. After shaking, set the test tube in the test tube rack and begin timing until the oil layer fully reappears in the tube. Record the time.
    After the reappearance of the oil layer, both layers will appear opaque due to the presence of small drops of the other substance suspended in the layers.

5. Repeat Step 4. Calculate the average time for the oil layer to reappear fully.

6. Repeat Steps 4 and 5 for Test Tubes 2–5.

7. In addition to the 50 drops added in Step 3, add 1 tsp dishwashing detergent to Test Tube 5. Repeat Steps 4 and 5 for this test tube.
    When the test tubes are emptied, the ones with the most detergent in them are cleaner and have fewer oil drops remaining in the container.

Variation

Perform this activity using several brands of dishwashing liquid. Make sure to keep the volumes of water and oil constant during each trial so the results can be compared. Also try liquid hand soap.

Discussion

- Ask students why the time required for the oil layer to reappear increases as more detergent is added to the test tube.
  As more detergent is added to the test tube, more and more oil becomes suspended in the soap micelles. The more oil suspended in the soap micelles, the longer it takes for the oil to come out of suspension and form a separate layer.

- Ask students to explain why detergents can clean greasy dirt from dishes.
  A detergent ion has a polar and a nonpolar end. The nonpolar ends of detergent can dissolve in grease droplets that are suspended in water during the washing process, forming micelles as described in the Explanation. The polar ends of detergent extend out of the micelles, causing these predominantly nonpolar entities to become soluble in water.

- Have students research recent oil spills. Discuss any spills that were cleaned up using detergents to break up the oil slick.

Explanation

Oil and water don't mix. When poured together, two separate layers form. Vigorous shaking does produce a temporary suspension of the oil and water. This suspension separates upon standing. Oils from plants and animals (e.g., vegetable oil, corn oil, and mink oil) make up a large class of molecules which are chemically similar to fats but most oils are liquid at room temperature. Oils are large molecules composed primarily of glycerides of fatty acids.

Water, on the other hand, is a very small molecule. (See Figure 1.) The oxygen and hydrogen do not equally share the two electrons making up each bond. This results in the oxygen retaining a slight negative charge and the hydrogens having a slight positive charge. This is what we mean by "polar."

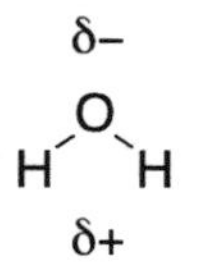

$$\delta-$$
$$O$$
$$H \quad H$$
$$\delta+$$

Figure 1: The structure of water

In contrast, fats and oils have bonds that are nonpolar because there is relatively little separation of charge in the carbon/hydrogen bonds. The separation of charge in water molecules causes them to attract each other strongly and cluster together in a layer. Since the water molecules are not strongly attracted to the oil molecules, the oil molecules separate from the water molecules, and two distinct layers are formed.

When detergent is added to the test tubes, the oil and water layers stay suspended for a longer period of time. The time required for the oil layer to reappear increases as more detergent is added. This phenomenon is due to the properties of soaps and detergents. Figure 2 shows the structure of sodium stearate, a common soap. Soap (and detergent) ions have two distinctly different parts. The long chain of carbon and hydrogen groups is referred to as the nonpolar tail and the charged group on one end is called the polar head.

H H H H H H H H H H H H H H H H H O
| | | | | | | | | | | | | | | | | ∥
H–C–C–C–C–C–C–C–C–C–C–C–C–C–C–C–C–C–C
| | | | | | | | | | | | | | | | | O⊖Na⊕
H H H H H H H H H H H H H H H H H

nonpolar tail   polar head

Figure 2: The structure of sodium stearate

The nonpolar tail is structurally similar to fats and oils, both of which contain large numbers of carbons and hydrogens. Because of this similarity, the nonpolar tail is attracted to fats and oils. However, the nonpolar tail is repelled by the polar water molecules. In water, the nonpolar tails of the soap cluster together forming a micelle. The amount or concentration of soap required for micelles to form is called the critical micelle concentration (cmc) and is usually quite small, typically around 0.01 molar (moles per liter of solution).

When the soap micelle encounters fats, oils, or grease, it absorbs the nonpolar material inside the micelle because of the "like dissolves like" attraction of the nonpolar species. Figure 3 shows the nonpolar part of the soap and the fat molecules inside the micelle and the charged, polar end of the soap exposed to the water. If large amounts of fats and oils are surrounded in this way, droplets of oil may remain suspended in solution and form visible suspensions. A suspension of a liquid in another liquid in which it is insoluble is called an emulsion. The detergent serves to promote the process of emulsification; it is an emulsifying agent. An increase in the solubility of oil in water is observed.

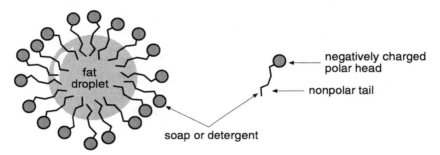

Figure 3: A cross-section of a simulated soap/oil micelle

Key Science Concepts

- chemistry of soaps and detergents
- emulsion
- polarity

Cross-Curricular Integration

Home, Safety, and Career
Prepare mayonnaise and challenge the students to explain why the oil does not separate from the mixture.

Mathematics
Have the students graph the average times for the five test tubes.

References

Alexander, A.; Bower, S. *Science Magic: Scientific Experiments for Young Children;* Prentice-Hall: New York, NY, 1986.

Allison, L.; Katz, D. *Gee Whiz! How to Mix Art and Science or the Art of Thinking Scientifically;* Little, Brown, and Company: Canada, 1983.

Herbert, D. *Mr. Wizard's Supermarket Science;* Random House: New York, NY, 1983.

Properties of Lubricants

When a liquid is "thick," it is said to be viscous, or to have a high viscosity. Is the liquid's high viscosity related to its density? In this activity, students explore these concepts.

Recommended Grade Level .... Part 1: 9–12; Part 2: 7–12
Group Size .... 1–4 students
Time for Preparation .... 10 minutes
Time for Procedure .... 40 minutes

Materials

Opening Strategy
- molasses
- clear glass graduated cylinder or measuring cup

Procedure
Per Class
- ice
- Styrofoam™ cooler
- hot plates
- balances
- paper towels
- marking pen or tape for marking cups
- dried empty bleach or milk jugs to use as waste containers for motor oil

Procedure, Part 1
Per Group
- alcohol thermometer
- 10-mL graduated cylinder
- 10 mL of a single-weight oil

➤ **Different groups can test different oil weights. Include at least SAE30, SAE40 (motor oils), and SAE90 (sold as gear oil for manual transmissions and differentials), which are available from most auto supply and discount department stores. Use additional weights if you can find them.**

Procedure, Part 2
Per Group
- 2 150-mL beakers
- 100-mL graduated cylinder
- long-stemmed funnel
- timing device with a second hand
- disposable cups
- 30 mL of a single-weight oil
- ring stand
- small ring clamp
- oven mitts

Variations

Per Group
- 3 25-mm x 200-mm screw-cap culture test tubes
- 3 plastic beads

Per Class
- 1-m sections of glass or rigid plastic tubing with an inside diameter of 8 mm (⅜ inch) that have been sealed on one end
- ball bearings to fit the tubes
- samples of some of the following liquids:
  - water
  - cooking oil
  - dishwashing detergent
  - corn syrup
  - molasses
  - rubbing alcohol
  - lubricating oil
  - various motor oils
- 2 magnets

Extensions

Per Class
- pancake syrup (regular and low-calorie)
- shampoo
- mineral oil
- liquid detergents, such as dishwashing liquid
- corn syrup
- glycerol
- vegetable oil
- rubbing alcohol
- 10W40 multiweight motor oil
- Emery Lubricant Emgard® E2811 synthetic lubricant
- 100-mL graduated cylinder

Resources

Screw-cap culture tubes can be purchased from a chemical supply company such as Fisher Scientific, 9403 Kenwood Road, Suite C-208, Cincinnati, OH 45242, 800/877-6658.

- culture tubes (25-mm x 200-mm)—catalog # 14-932F for 48 tubes

The Emery Lubricant Emgard E2811 can be obtained from Henkel Corporation, Emery Group, Attn: Jon Heimann, 4900 Este Avenue, Cincinnati, OH 45232, 513/482-4201.

The motor oils can be purchased at an auto supply store or discount department store.

Safety and Disposal

Do not heat the motor oil samples above 100°C because any water in the oil will boil and splatter the hot oil. Because the viscosity measurements do not alter the oil, samples of the oil can be used over again if students do not mix the various types. To dispose of the motor oil samples, collect the oil in jugs and take it to a recycling center or to a service station.

Getting Ready

Measure 20 mL water into a disposable cup. For each group, mark the sides of nine disposable cups at this height. These will serve as collecting cups. Measure 30 mL water into another disposable cup and mark three cups for each group at this height. These cups will be used for pouring each oil sample the first time. Dry the cups.

Opening Strategy

Explain to the students that lubricants (commonly called oil, grease, etc.) are used to reduce friction in and prolong the useful lifetime of machinery as well as to provide a seal between moving parts. Friction produces heat and wear and is undesirable in operating machinery. Liquid lubricants reduce friction by coating metal to prevent direct contact between metal parts. Moreover, oil, a widely used lubricant, removes heat from automobile engines and transfers it to the cooling system and keeps dirt and metal particles which wear off engine parts suspended until they reach the oil filter where they are trapped. Water is also carried away by the engine oil. In order to prevent corrosion, additives are usually put into oil. These additives react with corrosive compounds that form when the engine runs. Oil improves fuel economy (up to 5%) by helping to seal engine valves, where the fuel/air mixture is ignited. A pressure increase occurs during ignition and drives the piston. This pressure will be maximized if no gas can escape.

Ask the class "Now that you know what function a lubricant serves in machinery, what might be desirable properties of a lubricant?" *Thick (or slow-flowing), high boiling point, nonflammable, etc.* (If students do not mention thick or slow-flowing, lead them to mention this.)

Point out that one of the properties of lubricants that the students mentioned was thick or slow-flowing. Ask students if they have heard the phrase "As slow as molasses in January" (a phrase common in the cooler northern climates). Ask them to explain what that phrase means. Show them if they do not know. Place some molasses in a refrigerator or on ice and then pour the cold molasses from the bottle into a clear glass measuring cup until there is 100 mL of molasses in the cup. The students should see that molasses is highly viscous and, especially when it is cold, pours very slowly. Explain that this resistance to flow is called viscosity. If a liquid is to be used as a lubricant, its viscosity is important. Calculate the density of molasses by determining the mass of the 100 mL of molasses. The density is calculated by dividing the mass by the volume (g/mL). Explain that these two properties, density and viscosity, are characteristics of liquids that can be determined for any liquid.

Procedure

Part 1: Measuring Density

> Each group can be assigned a different oil sample to test. Each group of students should share their results with the rest of the class.

1. Determine and record the mass of a clean, dry, 10-mL graduated cylinder.

2. Pour exactly 10.0 mL of the oil sample into the cylinder and determine and record the mass of the liquid and cylinder. Subtract the mass of the empty cylinder from the total mass to determine the mass of the liquid.

3. Measure and record the temperature of the room.

4. Calculate the density of each liquid sample using the following formula:

$$density = \frac{mass\ of\ liquid\ (g)}{volume\ of\ liquid\ (mL)}$$

5. After calculating the densities of the oil samples, rank these densities from highest density to lowest density.

Part 2: Measuring Viscosity

> Each group can be assigned a different oil sample to test. Each group of students should share their results with the rest of the class.

1. Attach a small ring clamp to a ring stand. Place the funnel through the ring. Place a calibrated disposable cup underneath the stem of the funnel. (Use a new cup for each trial.) (See Figure 1.)

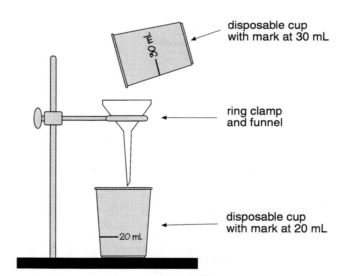

disposable cup
with mark at 30 mL

ring clamp
and funnel

disposable cup
with mark at 20 mL

20 mL

Figure 1: The apparatus used for the viscosity tests

2. Pour approximately 30 mL of the assigned oil sample into a calibrated pouring cup.

3. Quickly pour the oil sample into the long-stemmed funnel. Start timing as soon as you begin pouring. Determine and record the time required for the oil to reach the 20-mL mark on the side of the collecting cup.

4. Repeat Steps 2–3 twice and average your results for the latter two trials. (The funnel should have liquid on it previous to the trials that you use to average. The oil was not altered during the viscosity test, so the sample can be reused.)

 When heating the oil in the next step it is not important what the actual temperature is as long as it is known. DO NOT heat the oil samples above 100°C. Any water in the oil will boil and splatter the hot oil.

5. Using a hot plate, warm the beaker of oil to about 60°C.

 Wear oven mitts when removing the beaker of oil from the hot plate to protect your hands.

6. Remove the oil from the hot plate. Record the temperature of the oil directly before pouring it into the funnel.

7. Repeat Steps 2–4 twice for each sample of hot oil and record the results. Average the two trials.

 It may be necessary to heat the oil sample between trials.

8. Cool the oil to about 5°C by placing the beaker in ice water. Record the temperature of the oil directly before pouring it into the funnel.

9. Repeat Steps 2–4 twice for a sample of cold oil and record the results. Average the two trials.

Variations for Part 2

- Measure the viscosity of each oil sample by placing a sample of the oil and a plastic bead in a screw-cap culture test tube. (Fill tube to top.) Start by inverting the tube so the plastic bead is resting on the screw-cap. Turn the tube so the screw-cap is on top and time the bead as it falls. Temperature can be maintained by keeping the tubes in a hot-water bath or an ice bath. (The bead will move more slowly in a more viscous liquid and more rapidly in a less viscous liquid. See the *Chemistry in the Community* reference.)

- Measure viscosities by placing samples of different liquids such as water, cooking oil, dishwashing detergent, corn syrup, molasses, rubbing alcohol, and lubricating oil in 1-m sections of glass or clear rigid plastic tubing with an inner diameter of 8 mm (⅜ inch) that have been sealed on one end. Label each tube with the name of the liquid and tape the tubes to the wall or chalkboard so they are vertical. Drop identical-sized ball bearings into each tube and time the descent of the balls through the liquid. Rank the liquids in order from least viscous to most viscous. Remove the ball bearings with a magnet by moving the magnet upward along the outside of the tube. Two magnets may be needed to lift the ball bearings from the more viscous liquids. This procedure can also be used on different types of motor oils. (See "Viscosity Tubes" reference.)

Extensions

- Substitute different liquids for the single-weight motor oils used in the Procedure. Examples would be syrup (regular and low-calorie), shampoo, mineral oil, liquid detergents, corn syrup, and glycerol. You could also try various multiweight oils as well as synthetic lubricants (e.g., Emery Lubricant Emgard E2811).

- Prepare a density column by carefully pouring about 10 mL samples of various household liquids such as corn syrup (d=1.37 g/mL), dishwashing detergent (d=1.26 g/mL), water (d=1.00 g/mL), vegetable oil (d=0.91 g/mL), and rubbing alcohol (d=0.87 g/mL), down the side of a 100-mL graduated cylinder. Add the liquids in order of decreasing density. The syrup is very sticky and is better poured into the cylinder without allowing it to run down the sides of the cylinder. (See "Household Density Columns" reference.) However, a more engaging method of doing this extension is to use students' values for densities and see if they are right by whether liquids sink or lie on top of "more dense" liquids in the column.

Discussion

- Ask the students which oil sample was the most viscous and which one was the least viscous at room temperature, at about 0°C, and at about 60°C. Ask them what they noticed about the viscosity of the different oil samples at the different temperatures. *An oil becomes more viscous with decreasing temperature. This is why different oils are used in cars depending on the temperature or weather. Temperature is an important factor of viscosity. A single-weight oil such as the SAE30 will get much more viscous in cold temperatures. The multiweight oils (used in the first extension) such as the SAE10W40 are designed to have a larger range of temperatures where the viscosity will not change. For very cold temperatures, other oil products are used. The range of temperatures may not be large enough to detect a difference in viscosity of the multiweight oil.*

- Ask the students to construct a graph of density (y-axis) versus viscosity (the times for each liquid, x-axis) for the oil samples at room temperature and of viscosity (time for each liquid, y-axis) versus temperature (x-axis) for the individual oil they tested. Ask the students what the relationship is (if any) between density and viscosity for these oil samples and how temperature affects their viscosity. You may want to remind students that this relationship does not apply across different types of liquids. For example, water is denser than oil, but may very well be much less viscous.

Explanation

The resistance of a fluid to flow is called viscosity. High-viscosity fluids resist flow and are "thick" while low-viscosity fluids flow easily and are "thin." Proper viscosity is important for a lubricant, such as motor oil. Lubricants of low viscosity circulate easily in the engine and coat parts effectively at cold temperatures. High-viscosity lubricants protect engine parts better and make engines run more quietly. In the case of motor oils, it is desirable for them to have both kinds of viscosity characteristics.

Since a car's engine must function in a wide range of temperatures, the variation of viscosity with temperature is an important factor when deciding which motor oil to use. In general, the viscosity of pure fluids decreases as temperature increases. Because the viscosity should vary as little as possible with temperature, many motor oils are "blended."

Viscosity properties are specified by SAE (Society of Automotive Engineers) numbers. The higher the number, the higher the viscosity. Single-weight oils have one number, such as SAE30. Blended oils have two numbers, such as SAE10W40. The first number is the viscosity at

0°F and the second number is the viscosity at 210°F. The "W" stands for winter. Multiweight oils show much less change in viscosity with temperature than single-weight oils.

Motor oils can be made of natural oils or synthetic oils. Natural oils are high-molecular-weight organic compounds distilled from petroleum. Synthetic oils, like those produced by the Emery Group of Henkel Corporation, are essentially two different types of organic compounds, hydrocarbons and esters. For a more detailed explanation on the properties and chemistry of these different lubricants refer to the Content Review.

Density is a property of all matter. Every substance has its own characteristic density at a given temperature. The density of pure water is 1.0 g/mL at 4°C. The density of a liquid or solid will change slightly with changes in temperature. When most liquids and solids warm up, they expand, making the volume larger while the mass stays the same. This causes the density to decrease. (Water is unusual because, unlike most compounds, the solid form of water (ice) is less dense than the liquid because water expands when it freezes. From about 4°C to 100°C, water behaves as other liquids do.)

Key Science Concepts

- density
- properties of liquids
- viscosity

Cross-Curricular Integration

Mathematics
Have students graph the viscosity times versus the density of the oil samples.

Social Studies
Have students research the processing of petroleum and the variety of products made from petrochemicals.

References

American Chemical Society. *ChemCom: Chemistry in the Community,* 2nd ed.; Kendall-Hunt: Dubuque, IA, 1993; pp 160–162.

Guenther, W.B., "Density Gradient Columns for Chemical Display," *Journal of Chemical Education.* 1986, 63(2), 148.

"Household Density Column;" *Fun with Chemistry: A Guidebook of K–12 Activities;* Sarquis, M., Sarquis, J., Eds.; Institute for Chemical Education: Madison, WI, 1991; Vol. 1, pp 115–118.

"Looking at Motor Oil," *Science and Technology in Society, (SATIS),* The Association for Science Education: 1987; Unit 205.

"Make-It-Yourself Slime," *Fun with Chemistry: A Guidebook of K–12 Activities;* Sarquis, M., Sarquis, J., Eds.; Institute for Chemical Education: Madison, WI, 1992; Vol. 2, pp 67–75.

Sencen, J., *Chem 13 News.* May and September 1986, 15.

Tannenbaum, V., Fairfield High School, Fairfield, OH, personal communication, 1991.

"Viscosity Tubes;" *Fun with Chemistry: A Guidebook of K–12 Activities;* Sarquis, M., Sarquis, J., Eds.; Institute for Chemical Education: Madison, WI; Vol. 3 (in development).

Make-It-Yourself Slime

What is Make-It-Yourself Slime? In this activity, students make and study the properties of a polymer similar to the Slime® that you find in toy stores.

Recommended Grade Level 1–12
Group Size .... 1–4 students
Time for Preparation .... 20–45 minutes
Time for Procedure .... 30–45 minutes

Materials

Procedure

Per Group
- 5-oz plastic or paper cup
- stirring stick
- measuring spoon (1 Tbsp)
- graduated cylinder or measuring cup
- water-soluble marker
- small piece of paper or 3-in x 5-in index card
- zipper-type plastic bag

Per Class
- 1 L approximately 4% borax solution (sodium tetraborate, $Na_2B_4O_7$) made from the following:
  - 40 g (⅓ cup) laundry borax (sodium tetraborate decahydrate, $Na_2B_4O_7 \bullet 10\ H_2O$)
  - 1 L water
- 4% aqueous polyvinyl alcohol solution purchased or made as described in Getting Ready
- 2 1-L beakers or similar-sized containers
- stirring rod
- (optional) food color
- (optional) Lysol® Deodorizing Cleaner
- vinegar (in case of spills)

Extension

Per Group
- 0.75 g (¼ tsp) guar gum

Resources

Polyvinyl alcohol (99%–100% hydrolyzed with a molecular weight of 100,000) and guar gum (for the Extension) are available as a powder or as a 4% solution through Flinn Scientific, P.O. Box 219, Batavia, IL 60510-0219, 800/452-1261.

- polyvinyl alcohol (granular)—catalog # P0153 for 100 g

- 4% polyvinyl alcohol solution—catalog # P0210 for 1 L
- guar gum—catalog # G0039 for 100 g

Sodium tetraborate decahydrate solid used to make a 4% borax solution may be purchased at a grocery store as laundry borax.

Safety and Disposal

Some people have an allergic reaction to dry, powdered borax. As a result, care should be taken when handling it. Avoid inhalation and ingestion. Use adequate ventilation in preparing the borax solution and wash your hands after contact with the solid.

There is typically no danger in handling the Slime, but the students should wash their hands after use. Persons with especially sensitive skin or a known allergy to borax or detergent products should determine their sensitivity to the Slime by touching a small amount. Should redness or itching occur, wash the area with a mild soap and avoid further contact.

If the Slime spills on the carpet, apply vinegar on the spot and follow with a soap and water rinse. Do not let the Slime harden on the carpet. Do not set the Slime on natural wood furniture; it will leave a water mark.

Store the homemade Slime in a plastic bag. If you allow students to take the Slime home, send along a copy of the precautions and cleanup instructions from the preceding paragraphs. Discard Slime in a waste can or flush it down the drain with lots of water.

Any unused polyvinyl alcohol and sodium tetraborate solutions may be saved for future use or diluted with water and rinsed down the drain.

Getting Ready

Prepare an approximately 4% borax solution by mixing 40 g (⅓ cup) laundry borax (sodium tetraborate decahydrate, $Na_2B_4O_7 \cdot 10\ H_2O$) in 1 L water while stirring.

 Some people have an allergic reaction to the powdered borax. Use caution when handling.

Prepare an approximately 4% polyvinyl alcohol solution using one of the following methods:

a. Dissolve 40 g (⅓ cup) polyvinyl alcohol in 1 L water while stirring. Heat the mixture on a hot plate over moderately high heat, stirring constantly. The solution will initially be quite milky in color, but will clear when the polyvinyl alcohol is completely dissolved. The process may take up to 45 minutes. Cool the solution before using. If a slimy or gooey layer appears on the top during cooling, skim it off and discard it.

b. Dissolve 40 g (⅓ cup) polyvinyl alcohol in 1 L water in a microwave-safe container. Stir the mixture for about 2–3 minutes. Place it in a full-size microwave. Heat the solution on high for 8–10 minutes, stopping and stirring every 1–2 minutes to smooth the mixture, as you would do in making pudding. Adjust the time as needed to prepare.

Opening Strategy

The nature of polymer chains can be shown through this simple kinesthetic activity. Have 4–5 students stand in a line facing the class. Tell the class that each of these students represents a monomer. Have the monomers link arms or hold hands. Each pair of clasped hands represents a chemical bond. The chain they form is made of many units, simulating a polymer chain. Emphasize that polymers typically include hundreds or thousands of repeating units. Show the class how flexible the chain is by leading it around the room, weaving between the desks and chairs. Have another group of 4–5 students stand in a line and form another polymer chain parallel to the first chain. Have the chains move around as before. Note that the movement of one chain does not depend on the movement of any other unless the chains get very close to each other. Add crosslinkers between the polymer chains by assigning students not already in the chains to hold onto both chains at once. The movement of one chain now is influenced by the movement of others; the crosslinkers hold the chains together. Show this by having the chains try to move in the same direction. The crosslinkers will need to move also. Now have the chains move in opposite directions. The crosslink bonds must break from one of the chains. If the chains are moved back together, the crosslinks can reform in new places or in the same places.

Procedure

Part 1: Making the Slime

1. Pour approximately 30 mL (2 Tbsp) 4% polyvinyl alcohol solution into a cup.

2. (optional) Add a few drops of food color to the solution.

3. Observe the characteristics of the polyvinyl alcohol solution by stirring it with a stirring stick, examining the texture and viscosity.

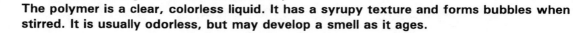

The polymer is a clear, colorless liquid. It has a syrupy texture and forms bubbles when stirred. It is usually odorless, but may develop a smell as it ages.

4. Pour 3 mL (½ tsp) 4% borax solution into the cup containing the polyvinyl alcohol solution. Stir constantly while adding borax solution.

5. Once the gel has formed, remove the Slime from the cup and knead it with your hands.

Part 2: The Characteristics of Slime

1. Experiment with the Slime that you prepared. Record any observations.

   - Squeeze it. What happens?

   - Form it into a ball and place it in the palm of your hand. What happens?

   - Drop the ball onto the table or bench. What happens?

   - Pull it first gently, then quickly. Does it react differently? If so, how?

   - Write your name with a water-soluble marker on a piece of paper or index card. Flatten out the Slime and press it to the name. What happens?

2. Store the Slime in a zipper-type plastic bag to prevent it from drying out. A few drops of Lysol Deodorizing Cleaner can be added to the Slime to minimize molding and extend the lifetime of the Slime.

Extension

- Repeat this activity using guar gum instead of polyvinyl alcohol. To make the guar gum solution for each group, mix 0.75 g (¼ tsp) guar gum in 80 mL (⅓ cup) hot tap water in a paper cup. Next add 30 mL (2 Tbsp) 4% borax solution while stirring the guar gum solution. It takes a few minutes for the gel to set. Compare the resulting Slime with the Slime made with polyvinyl alcohol.

Discussion

- Discuss why the polyvinyl alcohol solution got so thick after the borax solution was added.
  The borate ions act as crosslinkers between the polyvinyl alcohol chains. When the polyvinyl alcohol chains are immobilized, they trap water molecules between the chains and become a gel.

- Discuss the results of the tests done in Part 2.
  Slime has properties of both a solid and a liquid. It will bounce and stretch like a solid, but when it is placed on the table, it will flow like a liquid. Slime is classified as a non-Newtonian fluid which means it does not behave as most fluids do.

Explanation

In this activity you examined some of the properties of polymers (poly = "many" and mer = "units"). Polymers are formed by combining many repeating units called monomers (mono = "one"). Polymers are a group of molecules that play an important role in the world around us. Common polymers include plastics and many biological molecules such as proteins and carbohydrates.

The polyvinyl alcohol solution contains long polymer chains of polyvinyl alcohol that are dissolved in water. (See Figure 1.) Note that the alcohol groups (–OH) are on alternating carbons of the chain which may be several thousand carbon atoms long. Because these chains are very long, they interfere with each other's movement, causing this solution to be rather thick or viscous and to pour more slowly than water.

$$
\left[\begin{array}{cc} \overset{\displaystyle H}{\underset{\displaystyle H}{\overset{|}{\underset{|}{C}}}} & \overset{\displaystyle H}{\underset{\displaystyle OH}{\overset{|}{\underset{|}{C}}}} \end{array} \right]_n
$$

Figure 1: The repeating unit in polyvinyl alcohol

The Slime forms when the crosslinker, a 4% borax solution, is added. When borax (sodium tetraborate, $Na_2B_4O_7$) dissolves in water, it hydrolyzes to form a boric acid-borate buffer having a pH of about 9.

The borate ion becomes the crosslinker for the polymer chains. When added to the polyvinyl alcohol solution, the borate ions form crosslinks between different polymer chains as described in the equation shown in Figure 2. The borate ion is attracted to the alcohol groups (–OH) in the polyvinyl alcohol molecule within the polymer structure.

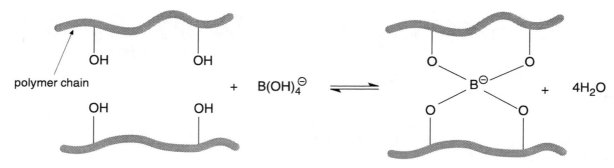

Figure 2: The reversible crosslinking of polyvinyl alcohol and the borate ion

However, due to certain properties of the polyvinyl alcohol-borate gel, it is probable that hydrogen bonding also has a role in the gel's formation. The structure shown in Figure 3 represents the possible hydrogen bonding in this situation.

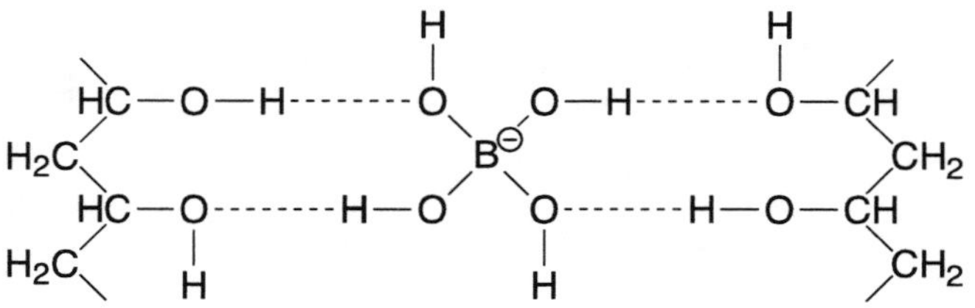

-------- = hydrogen bonds

Figure 3: Possible hydrogen bonding between polyvinyl alcohol and the borate ion

The crosslinking and hydrogen bonding shown in Figures 2 and 3 result in a three-dimensional network of polymer chains connected by borate. Water molecules occupy most of the space within the three-dimensional network that comprises the gel.

"Slime" belongs to a class of materials that do not obey the usual laws of physics, including viscosity, and are called non-Newtonian fluids. A low stress, such as slow pulling, allows Slime to flow and stretch and even form a thin film. A high stress, such as pulling sharply, will cause Slime to break. Hitting a piece of Slime lightly with a hammer will not cause splashing or splattering, and the material will even bounce to a small extent. If pushed through a tube, Slime will emerge with a swell (known as die swell in the plastics extrusion trade).

Key Science Concepts

- chemical reactions
- physical and chemical changes
- polymers and their properties
- scientific method

Cross-Curricular Integration

Language Arts
After making Slime, have students write about possible uses for such a product.

For younger students, relate the Slime in the activity to the tar in the book *Watch Your Step, Mr. Rabbit!,* by Richard Scarry (Random House, ISBN 0-679-81072-2). In this book, Mr. Rabbit gets stuck in tar. Try to relate the properties of Slimes to the properties of tar.

References

Casassa, E.Z., et al. "The Gelation of Polyvinyl Alcohol with Borax," *Journal of Chemical Education.* 1986, 63, 57–59.

Sarquis, A.M., "Dramatization of Polymeric Bonding Using Slime," *Journal of Chemical Education.* 1986, 63, 60–61.

"Make-It-Yourself Slime;" *Fun With Chemistry: A Guidebook of K–12 Activities;* Sarquis, M., Sarquis, J., Eds.; Institute for Chemical Education: Madison, WI, 1992; Vol. 2, pp 67–75.

Sarquis, A.M., et al. "Make-It-Yourself Slime;" *Science Activities for Elementary Classrooms;* Flinn Scientific: Batavia, IL, 1989; pp 39–42.

Selinger, B. *Chemistry in the Marketplace;* Harcourt Brace Jovanovich: Australia, 1988.

Woodward, L. *Polymers All Around You;* Terrific Science: Middletown, OH, 1992.

Other Books in the *Science in Our World* **Series:**

Science Fare—Chemistry at the Table (Procter & Gamble)

Dirt Alert—The Chemistry of Cleaning (Diversey Corporation)

Strong Medicine—Chemistry at the Pharmacy (Hoechst Marion Roussel, Inc.)

Chain Gang—The Chemistry of Polymers (Quantum Chemical Company)

Terrific Science Press
at the
Center for Chemical Education
Miami University Middletown

Terrific Science Press, Center for Chemical Education
Miami University Middletown
4200 E. University Blvd.
Middletown, OH 45042
513/727-3200
e-mail: cce@muohio.edu

ISBN 1-883822-09-2